LIVES OF GREAT RELIGIOUS BOOKS

The Tibetan Book of the Dead

LIVES OF GREAT RELIGIOUS BOOKS

The Tibetan Book of the Dead, Donald S. Lopez, Jr.

Dietrich Bonhoeffer's *Letters and Papers from Prison*, Martin E. Marty

Augustine's *Confessions*, Garry Wills

FORTHCOMING:

Revelation, Bruce Chilton

The Analects of Confucius, Annping Chin and Jonathan D. Spence

The Dead Sea Scrolls, John J. Collins

The Bhagavad Gita, Richard H. Davis

Josephus's *The Jewish War*, Martin Goodman

The Book of Mormon, Paul Gutjahr

The Book of Genesis, Ronald S. Hendel

The Book of Job, Mark Larrimore

The Greatest Translations of All Time: *The Septuagint* and *The Vulgate*, Jack Miles

The Passover Haggadah, Vanessa Ochs

The Song of Songs, Ilana Pardes

Rumi's *Masnavi*, Omid Safi

The I Ching, Richard J. Smith

The Yoga Sutras of Patanjali, David Gordon White

The Tibetan Book of the Dead

A BIOGRAPHY

Donald S. Lopez, Jr.

PRINCETON UNIVERSITY PRESS

Princeton and Oxford

Copyright © 2011 by Princeton University Press

Requests for permission to reproduce material from this work
should be sent to Permissions, Princeton University Press

Published by Princeton University Press, 41 William Street,
Princeton, New Jersey 08540

In the United Kingdom: Princeton University Press, 6 Oxford Street,
Woodstock, Oxfordshire OX20 1TW

press.princeton.edu

Library of Congress Cataloging-in-Publication Data

Lopez, Donald S., 1952–
    The Tibetan book of the dead : a biography / Donald S. Lopez, Jr.
        p.   cm.   — (Lives of great religious books)
    Includes bibliographical references and index.
    ISBN 978-0-691-13435-2 (hardcover : alk. paper)   1. Karma-
gliṅ-pa, 14th cent. Bar do thos grol.   2. Death—Religious aspects—
Comparative studies.   3. Future life—Comparative studies.
I. Title.
    BQ4490.K373L66 2011
    294.3'85—dc22   2010014137

British Library Cataloging-in-Publication Data is available

This book has been composed in Garamond Premier Pro
Printed on acid-free paper. ∞
Printed in the United States of America
10 9 8 7 6 5 4 3 2 1

My function, therefore, has been merely that of translator; all I have taken the trouble to do is adapt the work to our own habits. I have relieved the reader of oriental turns of phrase as far as I have been able to do so, and preserved him from countless lofty expressions, which would have bored him even in the clouds.

—Montesquieu, *Persian Letters*

CONTENTS

ACKNOWLEDGMENTS   ix

INTRODUCTION   1

CHAPTER 1   America   13

CHAPTER 2   India   30

CHAPTER 3   Tibet   49

CHAPTER 4   The World   71

CONCLUSION   128

CODA   153

NOTES   157

INDEX   171

ACKNOWLEDGMENTS

This book is my third encounter with *The Tibetan Book of the Dead*. The first occurred in 1998, when I devoted a chapter to it in *Prisoners of Shangri-La: Tibetan Buddhism and the West* (University of Chicago Press, 1998). The second occurred in 2000, when Oxford University Press republished the tetralogy of W. Y. Evans-Wentz, the first volume of which is *The Tibetan Book of the Dead*. I was invited to provide a new foreword for each of the four volumes, as well as an afterword for *The Tibetan Book of the Dead*. Although I provide a different perspective on the text here, much of the biographical information about Evans-Wentz presented in the following pages appears in these previous studies. The close reading of Evans-Wentz's text that occurs in chapter 4 is drawn largely from *Prisoners of Shangri-La*.

Acknowledgments, however, are typically a place to recognize the work of others. Here, I would like to direct readers interested in the history of the so-called *Tibetan Book of the Dead* in Tibet to the excellent study by Bryan J. Cuevas, *The Hidden History of the Tibetan Book of the Dead* (Oxford, 2003). In the course of writing this book, I have made consistent use of Bryan's study and pestered him with questions, all of which he has patiently answered.

The Tibetan Book of the Dead

In 2005, I received a telephone call from a newspaper in New Jersey. The journalist had seen a press release about a new translation of *The Tibetan Book of the Dead* and thought he might write a story about it. I referred him to a recently published scholarly study of the Tibetan text, but he wondered whether I could answer a few questions. "Is *The Tibetan Book of the Dead* the most important work in Tibetan Buddhism?" "No," I said. "Do all Tibetans own a copy?" "No," I said. "Have all Tibetans read it?" "No," I said. "Is it a work that all Tibetans have heard of?" "Probably not," I said. Before I had a chance to explain, the reporter, sounding somewhat bewildered, thanked me and hung up.

In his 1915 essay, "Thoughts for the Times on War and Death," Sigmund Freud wrote, "It is indeed impossible to imagine our own death; and whenever we attempt to do so we can perceive that we are in fact still present as spectators."[1] Four years later, the American Theosophist Walter Evans-Wentz, traveling in the Himalayas, chanced upon a Tibetan text and asked the English teacher of the Maharaja's Boarding School for boys in Gangtok, Sikkim to translate it for him. What is known in the West as *The Tibetan Book of the Dead* is the product of their collaboration.

The Tibetan work that was given this name by Evans-Wentz is one of many Buddhist texts known by the title *Bardo Tödöl* (in transliterated Tibetan, *Bar do thos grol*,[2] literally, "Liberation in the Intermediate State through Hearing"). It belongs to the genre of Tibetan literature called *terma* (*gter ma*) or "treasure." It is said to have been composed by the great Indian tantric master Padmasambhava, who visited Tibet in the eighth century. Knowing that his teachings would be needed in the distant future, he dictated books to his consort and scribe (the queen of Tibet) and buried them—sometimes in a cave, sometimes in a lake, sometimes in a pillar, sometimes in the heart of a disciple yet unborn—to await discovery when the time was ripe for their contents to be revealed to the world. He composed thousands of such works. The book called *Bardo*

Tödöl, buried in the eighth century, had been unearthed in the fourteenth century.

Evans-Wentz would discover that Tibetan text
in the twentieth century and, burying it under prefaces, commentaries, introductions, and annotations, he named it *The Tibetan Book of the Dead*.
Since its publication in 1927, the book has been discovered by millions of readers in the West who have
used it to do what Freud deemed impossible: imagine their own deaths.

Once it had appeared in English with this title,
The Tibetan Book of the Dead would go on to have
its own series of discoveries in the West, over the
course of almost a century. Seven major reincarnations (and several minor ones), seven discoveries of
this text, each somehow suited for its own time,
have occurred in English since 1919.[3] From the time
of its first incarnation in a Western language, *The
Tibetan Book of the Dead* has taken on a life of its
own as a timeless world spiritual classic. It is the first
Asian text, and the only Tibetan text, to have been
selected for inclusion in this series on the Lives of
Great Religious Books.

The worldwide fame of *The Tibetan Book of the
Dead*, regardless of the form the title has taken, derives directly from Evans-Wentz's volume, which
has served as the progenitor of the later versions, to

a greater extent than even the "original" Tibetan text. His book itself has had a number of reincarnations, in the form of editions, each with more and more prefaces and forwards added to the text. Since its publication by Oxford University Press, the various editions have sold over 500,000 copies in English; it has also been translated into numerous European languages.

Its full title is *The Tibetan Book of the Dead; or, The After-Death Experiences on the* Bardo *Plane, according to Lāma Kazi Dawa-Samdup's English Rendering.* It was "compiled and edited by W. Y. Evans-Wentz." This was the first of four books on Tibetan Buddhism that Evans-Wentz would produce, from translations made by others. In 1928, the year following the publication of *The Tibetan Book of the Dead,* Evans-Wentz brought out *Tibet's Great Yogī Milarepa* followed by *Tibetan Yoga and Secret Doctrines* in 1935, both based on translations by Kazi Dawa Samdup. The fourth and final work did not appear until much later. This was *The Tibetan Book of the Great Liberation*—based on translations done for Evans-Wentz by three Sikkimese—which was published in 1954.[4]

The first edition of *The Tibetan Book of the Dead* contained a "Preface to the First Edition" by Evans-Wentz as well as a foreword entitled, "Science of

Death" by Sir John Woodroffe, an official of the British Raj who during his time as Judge of the High Court of Calcutta had become a scholar and devotee of Hindu Tantra, publishing such works as *The Serpent Power* under the pseudonym Arthur Avalon. In addition, there was Evans-Wentz's own extensive introduction and copious annotations to Kazi Dawa Samdup's translation. The second edition (1949) included an additional preface by Evans-Wentz. The third edition (1957) brought the book close to the form in which it is best known today, adding a "Psychological Commentary" by C. G. Jung, translated by R.F.C. Hull from the original German version that appeared in *Das Tibetanische Totenbuch*, published in Zurich in 1935. The third edition also contained an Introductory Foreword by Lama Anagarika Govinda. Evans-Wentz added a preface to the first paperback edition (1960). And it was published yet again in 2000, "with a New Foreword and Afterword by Donald S. Lopez, Jr."

Thus, although the first sentence of Evans-Wentz's preface to the first edition reads, "In this book I am seeking—so far as possible—to suppress my own views and to act simply as the mouthpiece of a Tibetan sage, of whom I am a recognized disciple,"[5] the version of the book that we have today is filled with other voices (the various prefaces, introductions, forewords, commentaries, notes, and addenda comprise some two thirds of the entire book) that together overwhelm the translation. The increasing popularity of the work compelled this unusual assortment of authorities to provide their own explanation of the text.

This amalgam of commentaries, surrounding a translation of several chapters of a much larger Tibetan work, has become the most widely read "Tibetan text" in the West. Its appeal derives from the irresistible combination of two domains of enduring fascination: Tibet and death. At the time of the publication of *The Tibetan Book of the Dead*, Tibet, still a remote land in the high Himalayas, was regarded by many as a place where esoteric wisdom, long since lost elsewhere, had been preserved. Bounded on the south by the highest mountains in the world, at a time when mountains signified a cold and pristine purity, Tibet was imagined as a domain of lost wisdom. Tibet's geographical inaccessibility was not the only reason for this view. Of perhaps equal importance was the fact that Tibet had never come under European control, and as a result, many of the European fantasies about India and China, dispelled from these lands by colonialism, made their way across the mountains and became sited in an idealized Tibet. Evans-Wentz never entered Tibet, which in 1919 was largely inaccessible to Westerners. He remained instead on the borderlands, left to imagine what lay beyond the snowy range.

Even greater than the lure of Tibet is the eternal fascination with death. When Freud asserted that it is impossible to imagine one's own death, what he meant by death was the cessation of mental functions. But in the Buddhism of Tibet, consciousness never ceases, but passes through birth, death, the intermediate state or *bardo* (a Tibetan term that,as a result of Evans-Wentz's book, found its way into *Webster's Third New International Dictionary*), and rebirth, over and over again, until the achievement of buddhahood. Much of the allure of *The Tibetan Book of the Dead* can be attributed to the fact that it was the first work to offer an extended discussionof the Buddhist doctrine of death and rebirth toa large audience in the West, a doctrine elaborated in the Tibetan text with detailed descriptions of visions of peaceful and wrathful deities that appear in the nether world between death and birth. Thisvision of the afterlife found a ready audience during a different intermediate state, the period between the world wars. The late nineteenth century had been the heyday of Spiritualism, where mediums claimed to contact the spirits of the departed. Spiritualism experienced a revival after the First World War, when so many sought to know the fate of their lost fathers, sons, brothers, and husbands. Sir Arthur Conan Doyle, for example, turned to Spiritualism and sought to contact his son Kingsley, who died as a result of wounds suffered at the Battle of the Somme, while Freud wrote *Thoughts for the Times on War and Death* in 1915 as two of his sons served in the German army. The publication of *The Tibetan Book of the Dead* in 1927 preceded by two years the onset of the Great Depression, a period of profound anxiety in Europe and America about the future of the living. An ancient Tibetan text that described the post-mortem state in such precise and elaborate detail, and which explained that death was not an end, but a beginning, and that death was, indeed, an opportunity for enlightenment, offered both fascination and comfort.

Yet beyond the historical exigencies of its publication, *The Tibetan Book of the Dead* has proved remarkably resilient in subsequent generations, gaining far more readers in its English version (with subsequent translations into other European languages) than the Tibetan text—upon which it is based—ever had in Tibet. And it has been put to a remarkable range of uses. It inspired Timothy Leary,

Ralph Metzner, and Richard Alpert to publish *The Psychedelic Experience: A Manual Based on the Tibetan Book of the Dead* in 1964, a work in which the traditional teachings on the journey from one lifetime to the next were adapted into an instructional manual for an acid trip. Their book is largely forgotten today, except among true devotees of the Beatles, who know that the opening lines of "Tomorrow Never Knows" on the 1966 album *Revolver* come from this book, "Whenever in doubt, turn off your mind, relax, float downstream." In his 1966 recording, *OM*, John Coltrane and Pharaoh Saunders read aloud from *The Tibetan Book of the Dead*. In 1975, Stephen Levine and Richard Alpert, by now known as Baba Ram Dass and no longer an apostle of LSD, founded the Living/Dying Project in San Francisco, in which the dying were read passages adapted from *The Tibetan Book of the Dead*. In the 1990 film, *Jacob's Ladder*, a Vietnam veteran experiences disturbing hallucinations, and the viewer, like the protagonist, is unable to distinguish reality from illusion. At the end, it is revealed that the entire film has been the visions of an American soldier in Vietnam as he dies on the operating table. He is finally led into the light by a child. The director Adrian Lyne explained in interviews that the film had been inspired by *The Tibetan Book of the Dead*. Today, in addition to various translations, one can purchase an audio version of *The Tibetan Book of the Dead*, read by Richard Gere; a video dramatization of *The Tibetan Book of the Dead*, including film footage from Ladakh and an animated depiction of the state between death and rebirth, narrated by Leonard Cohen; *The Tibetan Book of the Dead for Reading Aloud* adapted by the playwright Jean-Claude van Italie; and a comic book version, *The Comic Bardo Thodol* by Thomas Scoville. An hour-long documentary on *The Tibetan Book of the Dead* aired in January 2007 as part of the History Channel's "Decoding the Past" series.

In a footnote to his introduction, Evans-Wentz writes that he and Kazi Dawa Samdup felt, "that without such safeguarding as this Introduction is intended to afford, the *Bardo Thödol* translation would be peculiarly liable to misinterpretation and consequent misuse ..." (1) They could have had little idea of the myriad ways in which their collaboration would be read. Removing the *Bardo Tödöl* from the moorings of language and culture, of time and place, Evans-Wentz transformed it into *The Tibetan Book of the Dead* and set it afloat in space, touching down at various moments in various cultures over the course of the past century, providing in each case an occasion to imagine what it might mean to be dead.

This book tells the strange story of *The Tibetan Book of the Dead*. It argues that the persistence of its popularity derives from three factors, two of which have been already mentioned. The first is the human obsession with death. The second is the Western romance of Tibet. The third is Evans-Wentz's way of making the Tibetan text into something that is somehow American.

Had the reporter stayed on the line with me in 2005, I would have explained why my answer to each of his questions was "no." I would have told him that the work by Walter Evans-Wentz entitled *The Tibetan Book of the Dead* is not really Tibetan, it is not really a book, and it is not really about death. It is about rebirth: the rebirth of souls and the resurrection of texts. Evans-Wentz's classic is not so much Tibetan as it is American, a product of American Spiritualism. Indeed, it might be counted among its classic texts. I would have told him that *The Tibetan Book of the Dead* is a remarkable case of what can happen when American Spiritualism goes abroad.

Like many tales, the tale I will tell involves a journey to strange lands with ancient masters, secret

teachings, and buried texts. But we sometimes for-
get that America has also been deemed sacred by
some, that American soil has also yielded sacred
texts. We will arrive in Tibet soon enough. But our
journey begins in America.

America

1816 was known in New England as the Year With No Summer. Temperatures plunged below freezing on June 5, July 6, August 13, 20, and 28. Eighteen inches of snow fell in Cabot, Vermont on June 7. Leaves froze, turned black, and fell from the trees. Crops failed, livestock died, people starved. Meteorologists now speculate that the terrible weather was caused by a cataclysm a world away, when Mount Tambora on the island of Sumbawa in the Indonesian archipelago erupted the year before, sending one hundred cubic kilometers of ash and pumice into the atmosphere. But many in New England saw the perversion of the season as a heavenly portent of a different sort; a mass migration occurred out of New England, with tens of thousands leaving their homes and farms for upstate New York, Ohio, and Michigan. Among them were

Joseph and Lucy Mack Smith, who left Norwich, Vermont with their eight children and moved to Palmyra, New York, where they opened a cake and beer shop. One of their children was Joseph Jr., born in 1805 in Sharon, Vermont.[1]

On the night of September 21, 1823, Joseph Smith, not yet eighteen, received a visitation from the angel Moroni in his family's farmhouse south of Palmyra, New York. Prior to his apotheosis as an angel, Moroni had been a mortal, a prophet, and a general of the Nephites, an Israelite tribe that had left Jerusalem and immigrated to the Americas in the sixth century BCE. After a devastating defeat by the Lamanites on the hill Cumorah in the fifth century CE (in what is today Ontario County, New York), Moroni fulfilled his father's instruction to complete the *Record of the Nephites*, which he inscribed on plates of ore and buried in a stone box on that hill. The angel Moroni appeared to Joseph Smith and told him where the plates could be found. He said, however, that Smith would only be able to take possession of the plates if he followed a number of commandments, including that he not use the plates for financial gain, that he inform his father of his vision of the angel, that he not let the plates touch the ground, and that he not show the plates to any unauthorized person.

Smith went to the hill Cumorah the next day and discovered the box, opening it to find the plates, as well as several artifacts, including two crystals, called the Urim and Thummim, set into a pair of spectacles. He removed the plates and set them on the ground beside him, but when he turned to look, they had disappeared and returned to the box. He tried to retrieve them, but was hurled to the ground by the angel. On the instructions of Moroni, he returned in consecutive years, on September 22, 1824 and 1825 but was unable to retrieve the plates. He returned yet again on September 27, 1827, this time with his bride Emma. He extracted the plates and the spectacles, and eventually brought them to the family farm. Smith did not permit others to see the plates, although he allowed selected family members and friends to hold them, wrapped in cloth. He described them as golden in color. Each plate was six inches wide and eight inches long, and was about the thickness of a sheet of tin. They were bound together by three rings into a book about six inches thick.

In October 1827, Smith and his wife moved to Harmony, Pennsylvania. They took the golden plates with them, in a glass box hidden in a barrel of beans. The angel Moroni had instructed Smith to translate the plates, and he began the process after settling in Harmony. Initially, he sat behind a curtain wearing the Urim and Thummim, which he called "the interpreters," and transcribed the characters he discerned on the plates. He soon began to translate them into English. His method was to put on the crystal spectacles and then place a stovepipe hat over his face; in some cases, he did not use the crystals but instead put a polished stone called a "seer stone" inside the hat. From the darkness, the text would appear in English, which he would read aloud for dictation. It appears that Smith was able to translate the inscriptions without placing the plates inside the hat; during much of the translation process, the plates remained hidden in the woods outside his house. Smith dictated the translation (the language of the inscriptions was later identified by Smith as "Reformed Egyptian") to his friend and benefactor, William Harris. After a substantial amount of translation (116 pages) had been completed, Harris convinced Smith to let him take the translation back to Palmyra, New York, where Harris apparently lost it.

Smith was distraught, and the angel briefly took away both the crystal spectacles and the plates. They were eventually returned on September 22, 1828 (the fifth anniversary of their discovery), and the translation project resumed at the point in the text where he had stopped with Harris, this time with Smith's wife Emma serving as the scribe (later replaced by Oliver Cowdery, a schoolteacher from Poultney, Vermont), and Smith using only the seer stone.

The translation was completed in Fayette, New York, where on June 11, 1829, Smith registered the title page for copyright at the local courthouse. The title was: *The Book of Mormon: An account written by the hand of Mormon, upon plates taken from the Plates of Nephi.* After showing the plates to eleven witnesses, Joseph Smith returned them to the angel.

Joseph Smith was not the only person to unearth ancient texts from American soil. On September 13, 1845, James Jesse Strang discovered the *Record of Rajah Manchou of Vorito* near Burlington, Wisconsin. Like Smith, he had been informed of its existence and location by an angel. He found a clay box buried under an oak tree, and opened it to reveal three tiny brass plates, only two and a half inches long and one and half inches wide, connected in a corner by a single ring. Two of the six sides had drawings, the other four were inscribed in an unknown script. Five days later, James Strang produced a translation, making use of crystal spectacles like those Smith had used. It read in part, "Record my words, and bury it in the Hill of Promise."[2]

Joseph Smith died in 1844. Almost four years later, on March 31, 1848, two sisters, Kate and Margaret Fox (ages ten and twelve), reported hearing rapping sounds coming from under the kitchen table in their family farmhouse in Hydesville, New York, only about ten miles east of where Joseph Smith had discovered the golden plates twenty years earlier. The girls soon developed a code by which they could communicate with the source of the raps, whom they first addressed as "Mr. Split-foot" (the Devil) and later identified as the spirit of a peddler who had been murdered in the house. With the support of a Quaker family in Rochester, the girls developed a following in the area and began communicating with the dead through séances in which they translated rapping sounds into the voices of the departed family members of their clients. With their older sister Leah acting as their manager, they became famous, attracting the attention of many of the leading figures of the day (with Horace Greeley, James Fenimore Cooper, and Sojourner Truth attending séances).

This interest in communicating with the dead, sparked by the Fox sisters, would come to be called "Spiritualism." It would continue throughout the nineteenth century and into the twentieth. In 1874, Henry Steel Olcott—a former journalist for Greeley's *New York Tribune*, a Civil War veteran, and attorney—went to Chittenden, Vermont to investigate paranormal events occurring in a farmhouse belonging to the Eddy brothers, who were said to be able to summon several spirits, including that of a Native American chief named Santum. There he met the Russian émigré and medium, Helena Petrovna Blavatsky. Their shared interest in Spiritualism, psychic phenomena, and esoteric wisdom led them to found the Theosophical Society in New York in 1875. The goals of the society included the formation of a universal brotherhood without distinction of race, creed, sex, caste, or color; the encouragement of studies in comparative religion, philosophy, and science; and the investigation of unexplained laws of nature and the powers latent in man. For Blavatsky and Olcott, Theosophy was an ancient wisdom that was the root and foundation of the mystical traditions of the world. This wisdom had been dispensed over the millennia by a group of Atlantean masters called *mahatmas*, or "great souls." In the modern period, these masters, seeking to escape the increasing levels of magnetism elsewhere in the world, had congregated in a secret location in Tibet. As Madame Blavatsky's disciple, A. P. Sinnett explained in *Esoteric Buddhism*:

> From time immemorial there had been a certain secret region in Tibet, which to this day

is quite unknown to and unapproachable by any but initiated persons, and inaccessible to the ordinary people of the country as to any others, in which adepts have always congregated. But the country generally was not in the Buddha's time, as it has since become, the chosen habitation of the great brotherhood. Much more than they are at present were the Mahatmas in former times distributed about the world. The progress of civilization, engendering the magnetism they find so trying, had, however, by the date with which we are now dealing—the fourteenth century—already given rise to a very general movement towards Tibet on the part of the previously dissociated occultists.[3]

Madame Blavatsky—who during her youth had spent summers in the Kalmyk region of Russia between the Black Sea and Caspian Sea, a region which had a large Mongolian Buddhist community—claimed that prior to coming to America she had studied under the tutelage of the mahatmas in Tibet over the course of seven years and that she remained in psychic communication with them— especially the masters Koot Hoomi and Morya— sometimes through dreams and visions, but most commonly through letters that either materialized in a cabinet in her room or which she transcribed through automatic writing. The mahatmas' literary output was prodigious, conveying instructions on the most mundane matters of the Theosophical Society's functions, as well as providing the content of the canonical texts of the society, such as A. P. Sinnett's *Esoteric Buddhism* and Madame Blavatsky's magnum opus, *The Secret Doctrine*.[4]

The Theosophical Society enjoyed great popularity in America, Europe, and India, playing an important but ambiguous role for Hindu nationalism in India and Buddhist nationalism in Sri Lanka. Its popularity continued after the death of Madame Blavatsky in 1891 and into the twentieth century, when her heir, Annie Besant, selected a young Hindu boy in 1909 as the messiah, the World Teacher, Krishnamurti. (Krishnamurti would renounce his divine status and break with the society in 1930.)

We will return to Joseph Smith, the Fox sisters, and Madame Blavatsky in the conclusion. But the stage for our exotic story is now set, and it is set in a very small, and decidedly unexotic, area of New York, New Jersey, and Vermont. Onto that stage enters the protagonist, Walter Evans-Wentz. He was born in Trenton, New Jersey on February 2, 1878, two hundred miles and fifty years from the place and time that the Angel Moroni restored the golden plates and crystal spectacles to Joseph Smith so that he could continue his work of translation; thirty years after the Fox sisters first heard the rappings; three years after Blavatsky and Olcott founded the Theosophical Society in New York City.

He was born simply Walter Yeeling Wentz. His parents were members of the Baptist Church of Trenton, but would break with the organized church to turn to Freethinking and Spiritualism. Young Walter also took an interest in Spiritualism, reading as a teen both *Isis Unveiled* and *The Secret Doctrine* by Madame Blavatsky. In 1894, he left high school after two years and began working as a journalist, after first taking courses in business in Trenton and in Jacksonville, Florida (where his family owned property). He eventually followed his family to southern California, where he joined the American Section of the Theosophical Society in 1901 at its headquarters in Point Loma, headed by Katherine Tingley, known as "the Purple Mother." He received a diploma from the Raja-Yoga School and Theosophical University in 1903. At Tingley's urging, he enrolled at Stanford, where he majored in English. In 1903, William Butler Yeats visited Stanford as part of his American tour. Inspired by

Yeats's lecture on Irish fairies, Wentz became interested in the influence of Celtic folklore on English literature. (Yeats had joined the Esoteric Section of the Theosophical Society in 1888, the same year he published *Fairy and Folk Tales of the Irish Peasantry*. He was expelled by Madame Blavatsky two years later.) In the spring of Wentz's senior year, 1906, William James was a visiting professor at Stanford. Wentz attended his lectures, perhaps finding in them confirmation of the Theosophical belief in a common core to religious experience. After earning an M.A. in English in 1907, Wentz went to Europe, studying Celtic folklore in the British Isles and in Brittany. He received the degree of *Docteur-ès-lettres* from the University of Rennes in 1909, and a Bachelor of Science in Anthropology from Oxford in 1910; one of his examiners was Andrew Lang. It was during this period that Walter Wentz, perhaps seeking to sound more British, began using his mother's family name and became Walter Evans-Wentz.

In 1911, Oxford University Press published Evans-Wentz's work on folklore, entitled *The Fairy-Faith in Celtic Countries*. It was dedicated to two Irish authors, each of whom had deep interests in Theosophy and the occult world. The first was George William Russell, a poet, painter, and Irish nationalist who published under the pseudonym Æ. The other was Yeats, "who brought to me at my alma mater in California the first message from Fairyland, and who afterwards in his own country led me through the haunts of fairy kings and queens." (One should not surmise from these dedications that all Irish writers of the period were devotees of Theosophy.[5])

The Fairy-Faith in Celtic Countries is a substantial work, containing two hundred pages of testimony: stories about fairies, trolls, and leprechauns recorded by Evans-Wentz during travels through Ireland, Scotland, Wales, the Isle of Man, Cornwall, and Brittany. This is followed by an "anthropological examination of the evidence," in which he identifies disembodied beings analogous to fairies in other cultures and religions. Here is an example of a story from Wales:

> A farmer went to Llangefni to fetch a woman to nurse his wife about to become a mother, and he found one of the *Tylwyth Teg*, who came with him on the back of his horse. Arrived at the farm-house, the fairy woman looked at the wife, and giving the farmer some oil told him to wash the baby in it as soon as it was born. Then the fairy woman

disappeared. The farmer followed the advice, and what did he do in washing the baby but get some oil on one of his own eyes. Suddenly he could see the *Tylwyth Teg*, for the oil had given him the second-sight. Some time later the farmer was in Llangefni again, and saw the same fairy woman who had given him the oil. "How is your wife getting on?" she asked him. "She is getting on very well," he replied. Then the fairy woman asked, "Tell me with which eye you see me best." "With this one," he said, pointing to the eye he had rubbed with the oil. And the fairy woman put her stick in the eye, and the farmer never saw again.[6]

The second section reconstructs the religion of the Celts, describing the pantheon of divinities as well as the underworld. Presaging the topic of his more famous work, Evans-Wentz focuses particularly on what he calls the doctrine of rebirth, which he finds not only among the Celts, but the Egyptians, Greeks, and Indians, as well as among the Druids, the Alexandrian Jews, and the early Church Fathers (then suppressed in the Middle Ages to be upheld only in secret by mystical philosophers and alchemists). For Evans-Wentz, the Celtic doctrine of rebirth represented an ancient form of Darwinism, yet one that surpasses Darwin because it provides "a comprehensive theory of man's evolution as a spiritual being both apart from and in a physical body, on his road to perfection which comes from knowing completely the earth-plane of existence."[7] Indeed, Evans-Wentz predicts that, "our own science through psychical research may work back to the old mystery teachings and declare them scientific."[8]

At the end of the book, Evans-Wentz considers various theories that might be put forward to explain away the existence of fairies—including pathology, delusion, and imposture—to conclude that, "(1) Fairyland exists as a supernormal state of consciousness into which men and women may enter temporarily in dreams, trances, and in various ecstatic states; or in an indefinite period at death. (2) Fairies exist, because in all essentials they appear to be the same as the intelligent forces now recognized by psychical researchers ..."[9] In the final chapter, he returns to the doctrine of rebirth, and the scientific evidence for it. Here, rebirth is evolutionary in character; it is impossible for a being to ever descend to a less advanced form—that of a plant or a brute animal, for example—after having previously passed through that stage of evolution.

This is the esoteric theory of evolution; any doctrines of rebirth that suggest anything different are a corrupt form, which he attributes to careless scribes and unscrupulous priests.[10] He concludes with a straightforward declaration of one of the fundamental tenets of Theosophy, without identifying it as such, calling it instead the "Celtic esoteric theory of evolution":

[T]here have been human races like the present human race who in past aeons of time have evolved completely out of the human plane of conscious existence into the divine plane of conscious existence. Hence the gods are beings which once were men, and the actual race of men will in time become gods. Man now stands related to the divine and invisible world in precisely the same manner that the brute stands related to the human race. To the gods, man is a being in a lower kingdom of evolution. According to the complete Celtic belief, the gods can and do enter the human world for the specific purposes of teaching men how to advance most rapidly toward the higher kingdom. In other words, all the Great Teachers, e. g. Jesus, Buddha, Zoroaster, and many others, in different ages and among various races, whose teachings are extant, are, according to a belief yet held by educated and mystical Celts, divine beings who in inconceivably past ages were men but who are now gods, able at will to incarnate into our world, in order to emphasize the need which exists in nature, by virtue of the working of evolutionary laws (to which they themselves are still subject), for man to look forward, and so strive to reach divinity rather than to look backward in evolution and thereby fall into mere animalism.[11]

After completing his thesis, Evans-Wentz began a world tour financed by the income he received from his family's rental properties in Florida. He was in Greece when the First World War broke out, and spent most of the war in Egypt, where he studied ancient Egyptian religion as well as Coptic Christianity. In 1917, he traveled to Sri Lanka and then to India, where he would spend the next five years.

We will also travel next to India, and not simply because Walter Evans-Wentz went there. His *Tibetan Book of the Dead* contains translations of Tibetan texts, texts said to have been composed by an Indian Buddhist master during his visit to Tibet in the eighth century. Thus, in order to understand those texts, and their teachings, we must return to India and its Buddhism. It is the ancient Indian Buddhist doctrine of rebirth—a doctrine rather different from the "Celtic esoteric theory of evolution"—that was transmitted to Tibet and which would find its way, with certain modifications, into the Tibetan text that Evans-Wentz encountered in 1919.

India

In ancient India, we cannot provide a standard chronology of an author's life and works. We encounter a different kind of evidence. The Buddha lived two and a half millennia ago, he wrote nothing during his life, his teachings were not committed to writing until some four centuries after his death, and biographies of the Buddha did not appear until after that. Scholars disagree about the dates of the Buddha's life, diverging in their opinions by a century. Even the length of the Buddha's life (eighty years) is mentioned in only one canonical text, the *Great Sūtra of the Final Nirvāṇa* (*Mahā-parinibbāna Sutta*), a work that likely dates from long after his death. We thus can know very little with historical certainty about the circumstances of the Buddha's life and the factors that led him to set forth his doctrines—it is even difficult to know which doctrines derive from him and which were ascribed to him over the subsequent centuries.

Buddhism had all but disappeared from India by the fourteenth century, and the evidence that survives, largely in the form of texts preserved in Indic languages or translated into Chinese and Tibetan, tell us much about philosophical doctrine and meditation practice; they tell us little that is reliable about the authors of the texts and the lives they lived. We shall return in the conclusion to this question of the historical record and its implications for religious authority. In this chapter, I will describe Indian Buddhist views of death and rebirth, especially those that proved to be important in Tibet.

From the texts of Indian Buddhism, a view of life and death emerges that has remained relatively consistent across the history and geography of the Buddhist world. Here, the Buddha explained that the beings of the universe wander through the realms of rebirth. This cycle, called *saṃsāra* in Sanskrit (literally "wandering") has no beginning and also no end, except for those fortunate beings who successfully traverse the path to nirvāṇa, the state of eternal freedom from birth and death. Until then, beings are born again and again, into one of six realms: as gods, demigods, humans, animals, ghosts, or hell beings. These realms are most elaborate above and below, with a variety of heavens located on a central mountain and in the skies above it, and a variety of hells—both hot and cold—located deep beneath the surface of the earth. Each of these states (including that of the gods) is a temporary abode of varying lifespan, ending in death and then rebirth. The realms of animals, ghosts, and hell beings are regarded as places of great suffering, whereas the godly realms are abodes of great bliss. Human rebirth falls in between, bringing, as it does, both pleasure and pain.

The engine of saṃsāra is fueled by karma, the cause and effect of actions. Like other Indian religions, Buddhist doctrine holds that every intentional act, whether physical, verbal, or mental, leaves a residue in its agent. That residue, like a seed, will eventually produce an effect at some point in the future, an effect that takes the form of pleasure or pain for the person who performed the act. Thus, Buddhists conceive of a moral universe in which virtuous deeds create experiences of pleasure and non-virtuous deeds create experiences of pain. These latter are often delineated in a list of ten non-virtuous deeds: killing, stealing, sexual misconduct, lying, divisive speech, harsh speech, senseless speech, covetousness, harmful intent, and wrong view. The first three of these are negative deeds of the body, the next four are negative deeds of speech, the last three are negative deeds of the mind. Thoughts, both positive and negative, can produce karmic effects in the future. Buddhist texts provide extensive discussions of the specific deeds that constitute these ten non-virtues and their respective karmic weight.

These deeds not only determine the quality of a given life but also determine the place of rebirth after death. Depending on the gravity of a negative deed (killing being more serious than senseless speech and killing a human more serious than killing an insect, for example) one may be reborn as an animal, a ghost, or in one of the hot or cold hells, where the life span is particularly lengthy (millions of years). Among the hells, some are more horrific than others; the most tortuous awaits those who have committed one of five heinous deeds: killing one's father, killing one's mother, killing an arhat (someone who has achieved nirvāṇa), wounding a buddha, and causing a schism in the community of monks and nuns.

Rebirth as a god or human is the result of a virtuous deed, and is considered very rare; the vast majority of beings in the universe are said to inhabit the three unfortunate realms of animals, ghosts, and the hells. Rarer still is rebirth as a human who has access to the teachings of the Buddha. In a famous analogy, a single blind tortoise is said to swim in a vast ocean, surfacing for air only once every century. On the surface of the ocean floats a single golden yoke. It is rarer, said the Buddha, to be reborn as a human with the opportunity to practice the dharma than it is for the tortoise to surface for its centennial breath with its head through the hole in the golden yoke. The message, of course, is that human birth with access to the Buddha's teachings is precious and rare, not to be squandered.

Despite the fame of nirvāṇa, most Buddhist practice has historically been directed not toward this state of final liberation from rebirth but toward a happy state within the realm of saṃsāra, with the realm of gods regarded as a desirable destination. Rebirth as a god is said to be the result of deeds of generosity in a former life, with the order of Buddhist monks regarded as a particularly efficacious recipient of such charity. Rebirth as a human is said to be the result of ethical deeds, with the observance of vows not to kill, steal, lie, engage in sexual misconduct, or use intoxicants regarded as particularly efficacious.

Images of the Buddhist afterlife, particularly in East Asia, often depict the spirit of the deceased standing before a judge, with its good and evil deeds being weighed on a scale; such a scene occurs in the *Bardo Tödöl*. However, according to classical doctrine, one's next rebirth is not determined by the cumulative weight of good or evil deeds performed in this life. Rather, a single deed performed in any past life from the incalculable past (technically, any "complete action" in which the intended deed is carried out to completion) can serve as the cause for an entire lifetime. Which one of that infinite number of deeds—their karmic seeds all preserved in the mind—comes to the fore to create the next lifetime is said to be determined by the state of mind at the moment of death. Thus, there are instructions in all Buddhist cultures on how to prepare for death, instructions both for the friends and family at the deathbed as well as for the person who will soon begin the journey to the next lifetime. Although these instructions vary from culture to culture, in general, they seek to promote positive states of mind (such as devotion to the Buddha) and reduce negative states of mind (such as attachment to possessions and loved ones). If a positive state of mind is present at the moment of death, it is said that a virtuous deed (done at some point in the past) will serve as the cause of the next lifetime, and the person will be reborn as a human or a god. If a negative state of mind is present at the moment of death, a non-virtuous deed from the past will serve as the cause of the next lifetime, and the person will be reborn as an animal, ghost, or hell being. After death, it is said that one is blown by the winds of one's own karma to the next lifetime.

In a system that seems so mechanical (in its own way), one might imagine that there would be no possibility of navigating those winds, no means of intercession through prayers and good deeds done on behalf of the dead. One would be wrong. A wide variety of rituals are performed across the Buddhist world on behalf of the dead; performing such rituals has long been a primary occupation of the Buddhist priest (whether lay or monastic). Indeed, the Tibetan works dubbed *Bardo Tödöl* are motivated by the belief that the deceased can receive valuable instructions in the post-mortem state. However, before examining how such instructions are provided, it is important to define death, rebirth, and what happens in between more precisely.

Tibet received from Indian Buddhism an elaborate system of human physiology, according to which much of what would be thought of today as the autonomic nervous system is described as a network of 72,000 channels, through which subtle energies called winds (*rlung* in Tibetan, *prāṇa* in Sanskrit) flow. These winds make possible all forms of physical function, including breathing, digestion, and orgasm. Among the channels, the most important is the central channel, which runs from the genitals upward to the crown of the head, then curving down (according to some systems) to end in the space between the eyes. Parallel to the central channel are the right and left channels, which wrap around it at several points, creating constrictions or knots that prevent wind from flowing through the central channel. At these points of constriction, there are also networks of smaller channels that radiate throughout the body. These points are called wheels (*'khor lo, cakra*), often enumerated as seven: at the forehead, the crown of the head, the throat, the heart, the navel, the base of the spine, and the opening of the sexual organ. The winds that course through the channels are said to serve as the vehicles or "mounts" of consciousness. The most subtle form of consciousness resides in the heart wheel. It is called the mind of clear light.

The process of death is described as the gradual withdrawal of the winds from the channels that run throughout the body, and the attendant failure of physical and sensory function, as the winds withdraw from the network of channels and begin to gather in the central channel. This occurs over what are called the eight dissolutions. In the first dissolution, the body becomes weak, vision becomes dim; unable to open or close the eyes, one feels as if one is sinking, and there is a vision of a mirage. In the second dissolution, all physical sensation is lost, the mouth becomes dry, one loses the ability to hear, and there is a vision of thick smoke. In the third dissolution, one can no longer remember the names of friends and family, the warmth of the body begins to diminish, digestion becomes impossible, inhalations become short and exhalations become long, one can no longer smell, and there is a vision of fireflies. In the fourth, breathing stops, one loses the senses of taste and touch, one is unaware of one's circumstances, and there is a vision of a sputtering butter lamp.

By the time of the fifth dissolution, all five of the senses have ceased to operate. At this point, various emotional states, known as the eighty conceptions, dissolve. The winds from the channels that course through the upper part of the body have further withdrawn from the right and left channels and have gathered at the crown of the head at the top of the central channel. When these winds descend through the central channel toward the heart wheel, what appears to the mind of the dying person changes from a burning butter lamp to a radiant whiteness, a color described as being like that of a clear autumn night just before dawn, with the sky pervaded by moon-light. This appearance of whiteness is caused by the downward movement of the white drop received from the father at the moment of conception. In the sixth dissolution the winds from the lower part of the body enter the center channel at the base of the spine and ascend toward the heart. This produces an appearance of a bright red color, like a clear autumn sky pervaded by sunlight. This appearance of red-ness is caused by the upward movement of the red drop received from the mother at conception. The red and the white drops (and their attendant winds) surround what is called the indestructible drop lo-cated in the center of the heart wheel. This drop, said to be the size of a small pea, white on the top and red on the bottom, encases the most subtle wind and the most subtle form of consciousness, the mind of clear light. At the seventh stage, the winds that have gathered above and below enter into the heart wheel, bringing about an appearance to the dying person of radiant blackness, like a clear autumn sky in the evening after the sun has set and before the moon has risen, pervaded by thick darkness. Here, it is said that the dying person loses mindfulness, swooning in the darkness into unconsciousness. Fi-nally, in the eighth stage, the mind of clear light dawns, with the appearance of the natural color of the sky at dawn, free from sunlight, moonlight, and darkness. This is death.

The consciousness of the deceased then departs from the body and sets out for the next lifetime. Some texts describe the consciousness exiting from different places depending upon its destination: from the anus for those who will be reborn in hell, from the mouth for those who will be reborn as ghosts, from the urinary passage for those who will be reborn as an animal, from the eye for those destined to be reborn as a human, from the navel for those who will be reborn in heaven as a god.

Buddhist schools disagree on how long it takes to arrive at the place of rebirth. According to the Theravāda tradition of Sri Lanka and Southeast Asia, rebirth is immediate. However, other Indian schools, including those that spread to Tibet and East Asia, argue that it is not possible for a cause to produce its effect at a distant place and time; in order for a grain of rice grown in one village to take root and bear fruit in another village, it must be physically transported to the new place; there must be an unbroken continuity between cause and effect. Thus, they describe the existence of something called the *antarābhava*, literally, the "between existence," more commonly translated as the "intermediate state." The term is better known in its Ti-

betan translation, *bar do*, literally "between two."
According to this view, the consciousness of the deceased enters into this new existence by passing once again through the visions that preceded death, but in reverse order—clear light, radiant blackness, radiant redness, radiant whiteness, butter lamp, fireflies, smoke, and mirage—and is then reborn in the intermediate state, with unusual features. The "bardo being," as it is sometimes called, is born spontaneously and fully formed, without gestation, with all sense organs functioning from the moment of birth. Although it has a subtle body, not one made of coarse matter, it has the shape of the body it will soon assume in the next lifetime; if it is to be reborn as a human, it will have the form of a human, if it will be reborn as a dog, it will have the form of a dog. However, the texts specify that its body will be that of a being of five or six years old (presumably, this pertains to humans, and the requisite number of "dog years" would pertain in the case of canines). According to the classical presentation of the intermediate state, it is not possible to change one's destiny there—that is, a being destined for rebirth as an animal cannot be reborn as a human. This is because a single karmic cause creates both the being of the intermediate state and the being of the next lifetime.

The color of the body also depends upon its future destiny. If it is impelled by positive deeds toward a good rebirth, the body is the color of moonlight. If it is impelled by negative deeds toward a bad rebirth, the body is the color of dark clouds; another text provides more detail, saying that those destined for hell will have a body that is the color of a burned tree stump. Future ghosts will be the color of water and future animals will be the color of smoke. Those destined for rebirth as a human or a god will have a golden body. The bardo being does not require food, instead consuming fragrances, either pleasant or unpleasant depending on its past karma. It neither casts a shadow nor leaves a footprint, and, though it may call out to humans, its voice cannot be heard. The bardo being can see other beings of its own class—in other words, beings destined for rebirth as an animal can see other beings who will be reborn as animals. Yet all bardo beings can be seen by those beings who, through yogic practice, have gained the "divine eye," the ability to see things that others cannot. It is also said that beings destined for a lower rebirth experience visions of darkness; those destined for a higher rebirth experience visions of light.

The bardo being is able to travel at great speed,

unimpeded by any physical obstacle, even a mountain (except Vulture Peak, where the Buddha set forth so many sūtras). If it is destined for rebirth in hell, there is a sense of descending. Those beings who will be reborn as a ghost or animal feel they are traveling over a flat plain. Those destined for rebirth as a human or a god have a sense of ascending. The only thing that can block its movement is the womb of its future mother. The bardo being can live as long as seven days in the intermediate state. If it has not found a place of rebirth by then, it suffers a "small death," being reborn again in the intermediate state. It can survive in the intermediate state for seven of these seven-day periods; it will inevitably find a place of rebirth in forty-nine days.

By the end of forty-nine days, if the bardo being is to enter a womb (rather than be reborn spontaneously as god, ghost, or hell being), it is driven by the desire for sexual intercourse, arriving at the place where its future parents are copulating. If it is to be reborn as a male, it will feel desire for the future mother and hatred for the future father. If it is to be reborn as a female, it will feel desire for the future father and hatred for the future mother. It is a moment of hatred that kills the bardo being, bringing an end to life in the intermediate state and the beginning of the next lifetime. Consciousness departs the bardo being and enters the fertilized ovum. This is the process of rebirth in saṃsāra.

The ultimate goal of Buddhist practice is to escape from saṃsāra, to put an end to the process of birth, death, and rebirth. In early Buddhism, this was achieved by gaining insight into the nature of reality (usually described as the absence of a permanent and independent self). Such insight not only prevented the production of the karmic seeds for future birth, but also destroyed the seeds of all past deeds. The destruction of the seeds for future rebirth could take place over several lifetimes, over the course of one lifetime, or in a single session of meditation (as the Buddha did on the night of his enlightenment). With the seeds of all future rebirth destroyed, when the causes of the present life were expended, one would die and never be reborn again. One would not be reborn because there was nothing to be reborn. By eliminating the causes of rebirth, rebirth became impossible, resulting in the cessation of consciousness called nirvāṇa.

With the rise of the Mahāyāna near the beginning of the Common Era, some four centuries after the Buddha's death, nirvāṇa came to be reinterpreted not as the cessation of consciousness, but its purification. Buddhahood came to be seen as a permanent state of omniscience, with the appearance of the Buddha on earth as simply an emanation of this principle of enlightenment, teaching the dharma out of compassion for the world. Thus the Buddha did not die and pass into nirvāṇa at the end of eighty years. He only appeared to do so. In reality, the Buddha had been enlightened eons before. Yet in order to inspire the world, he pretended to be reborn as a prince; he pretended to live the life of luxury in the palace; he pretended to take four chariot rides outside the palace when he was twenty-nine, encountering an old man, a sick man, a corpse, and a meditating mendicant; he pretended to leave the palace to practice asceticism for six years; he pretended to achieve enlightenment under the Bodhi Tree; he pretended to pass into nirvāṇa. All of this was the Buddha's compassionate display. In fact, he was enlightened long ago. In fact, he will never die. The goal of Buddhist practice, then, was no longer the permanent cessation of consciousness called nirvāṇa, but rather the immortality and omniscience of buddhahood.

Some four centuries after the rise of the Mahā-yāna, tantric Buddhism developed in India, and the doctrine of the intermediate state began to take on a new importance. The intermediate state was portrayed not simply as a kind of limbo to be endured between one lifetime and the next, but as an opportunity for the vital transformation of consciousness that results in buddhahood. This new role for the intermediate state developed in part from an emphasis on the mind of clear light, the most fundamental form of consciousness, which when fully manifested and recognized, served as the foundation of enlightenment. This mind of clear light did not become manifest only at the conclusion of the series of dissolutions that marked the end of one lifetime and the beginning of another. Death and rebirth were occurring constantly. The mind of clear light became manifest every night as one fell asleep and took on a new form in a dream, and became manifest again as the dream ended and one resumed one's waking form.

Thus, among the six yogas of Nāropa, teachings associated with a famous eleventh-century Bengali scholar and yogin, we find the practices of "dreams," "clear light," and "intermediate state." The last seeks to transform the three stages of death, intermediate state, and rebirth into buddhahood, turning death into the Truth Body (*dharmakāya*) of the Buddha, the intermediate state into the Enjoyment Body (*saṃbhogakāya*) of the Buddha, and rebirth into the Emanation Body (*nirmāṇakāya*) of the Buddha. That is, at the moment of death, the mind of clear light would be transformed into the omniscient consciousness of a Buddha, called the Truth Body. Rather than entering the body of a bardo being, it would emerge in the form of the Enjoyment Body. Then, rather than traveling through the intermediate state to be reborn yet again in saṃsāra, the Enjoyment Body would manifest in the world as an Emanation Body of the Buddha.

From the perspective of the tantric tradition, this is the most advanced form of Buddhist practice. It involves initiation, followed by detailed visualizations of maṇḍalas—divine palaces inhabited by buddhas, bodhisattvas, and deities—followed by yogic practices that cause the winds to enter the central channel and the mind of clear light to become manifest. The important point, however, is that in Buddhist tantra, the stages of death and rebirth became transformed from largely mechanical processes driven by past karma into rare opportunities for the achievement of buddhahood in the here and now. Indeed, in his "yoga of the intermediate state," Nāropa speaks of three such states, the intermediate state between birth and death, the intermediate state between sleep and dream, and the intermediate state between death and rebirth. From this perspective, the intermediate state encompasses all moments of existence, for we are always in between two states. The intermediate state, the bardo, thus came to represent ever proliferating periods of transition from one state to another, liminal spaces that serve as the site for realization. It is this science of birth, death, and rebirth that would be transmitted from India to Tibet.

Tibet

According to a well-known myth, the first Tibetan kings descended from heaven by means of a rope. When the king's firstborn son had reached maturity (measured by the ability to master a horse), the king would return to heaven via the rope, never to be seen again. The departed king disappeared like a rainbow, leaving no corpse behind. The first seven kings of Tibet descended and ascended in this way. The eighth king bore the ominous name Ti-gum (Gri gum), "Killed by the Sword." Knowing his fate, the king challenged his groom to a duel, and sent a spy to determine how the groom would arm himself. The groom, recognizing the spy, deceived the king by musing aloud, "If the king binds a black leather turban on his head, fastens a mirror on his brow, carries the corpse of a fox on his right shoulder and the corpse of a dog on his left, loads and binds leather bags of dust on a hundred red oxen and cows, and brandishes the sword called Lang-ja-po (Glang bya pho, 'Male Ox Bird') over his head, I am no match."[1] On the windswept field of battle, the groom immediately slashed open the bags of dust on the backs of the oxen, creating a blinding dust storm. Waving his sword wildly above his head in the confusion, the king inadvertently cut the heavenly cord. Because he had dead animals affixed to his shoulders, his protective deities would not approach to defend him. Although difficult to discern the king in the dust, the groom saw the sun reflect off the mirror in the king's turban, drew his bow, and loosed a fatal arrow. And so the royal funerary cult began.

Like all cultures, Tibet developed practices for the disposal of the dead, including cremation, burial, mummification, and chopping up the body and feeding it to birds, the so-called "sky burial." But with the introduction of Buddhism, the ideology reflected in these practices was that of rebirth in the six realms of saṃsāra, and the ultimate goal of putting an end to rebirth in nirvāṇa.

According to Buddhist legends, Buddhism entered Tibet during the reign of the twenty-eighth king (who likely lived in the fifth century CE). By this time, Tibet was surrounded by Buddhist cultures: India and Nepal to the south; Kashmir and Afghanistan to the west; China to the east. Yet, according to the story, Buddhism entered Tibet from none of these directions, arriving instead from above, when a casket of texts fell onto the roof of the royal palace. The king opened the casket and examined the texts, but finding them illegible (Tibet had no written language at this time), he resealed the casket, dubbed it the "Sacred Secret" and left it for future generations to read. Five generations later, in the seventh century, the thirty-third king of the dynasty, Songtsen Gampo (Srong btsan sgam po), received Buddhism from the east and south. As a result of treaties, he accepted as wives first a Nepalese princess and then a Chinese princess. Both were Buddhists, and they converted their husband. He built temples in Lhasa to house the statues of the Buddha they had brought from their homelands, and he sent a delegation to India to learn Sanskrit and then return to invent an alphabet for Tibetan so the teachings of the Buddha could be translated. And so began what the Tibetans call the "early spreading of the dharma."

The building of temples and the translation of texts began in earnest under the patronage of the thirty-eighth king, Trisong Detsen (Khri srong lde btsan), who ruled the Tibetan empire over the last half of the eighth century. In order to establish the first Buddhist monastery in Tibet, he invited the great Bengali master Śāntarakṣita, former abbot of the great Nālandā monastery in northern India. Impeded by various natural disasters and the protestations of local priests, he urged the king to invite a renowned tantric master named Padmasambhava ("Lotus Born") from India (he is said to have come from Oḍḍiyāna, traditionally identified with the Swat Valley in what is today northern Pakistan), who would be able to dispel the obstacles to the monastery's establishment. Padmasambhava accepted the invitation and succeeded in subduing the local spirits. Together, the king, the abbot, and the adept, founded Samye (Bsam yas), the first Buddhist monastery, and seven Tibetans were ordained as the first monks. Buddhism flourished, and more monasteries were founded, numerous masters were invited from India, and hundreds of Sanskrit sūtras were translated into Tibetan. Royal patronage of Buddhism came to an end with the ascent of the evil king Lang Darma (Glang dar ma), who is said to have closed monasteries and defrocked monks and nuns. He was assassinated by a Buddhist monk in 842, and the Tibetan monarchy came to an end.

According to later historians, Tibet plunged into almost two centuries of political chaos and religious corruption, which ended only when a pious prince in western Tibet sought to restore the dharma by sending a group of twenty-one young men into India to bring back Buddhism (only two returned alive) and by inviting the renowned Bengali scholar Atiśa to come from the monastery of Vikramaśīla. These events mark for the Tibetans the beginning of the "later spreading of the dharma." This period was one of extensive spiritual traffic between India and Tibet, with Tibetans making the perilous trip across the Himalayas, returning as tantric initiates bearing texts and lineages. As Buddhist institutions in India came under threat from Muslim armies, Indian masters also made the journey north. The major sects of Tibetan Buddhism arose during this period. These were the Kadam (Bka' gdams) associated with Atiśa; when Tsong kha pa established what came to be known as the Geluk (Dge lugs) in the fifteenth century, he called it the "new Kadam." The Kagyu (Bka' brgyud) traced its origins to the three trips made to India by Marpa the Translator, the teacher of Milarepa. (It is noteworthy that both of these sects employ the term *bka'* or "speech" in their names, evoking their claim to direct oral instruction from Indian masters.) The third was the Sakya (Sa skya), which traced its teachings to the Indian master Virūpa, and was named after its chief monastery, "Gray Earth" (*sa skya*). The fourth sect called itself "Ancient" (Rnying ma). It did not trace itself to pilgrimages to India or recently arrived Indian masters. It did not invoke oral instructions passed from master to disciple, unbroken by the passage of time. Instead, it looked to the distant past and to the written word.

The history of the ancient kings described here was not recorded until centuries after the events it claims to recount, and subsequent scholarship has called into question the existence of the Nepalese princess, as well as the piety of Songtsen Gampo. It is unclear whether Padmasambhava was a historical figure; recent scholarship suggests that, if he was, his contribution to Tibetan culture was the introduction of certain irrigation techniques. But for reasons that are not entirely clear, over the subsequent centuries, he underwent an apotheosis, transformed into the "Precious Guru," by far the most famous of the Indian masters who may have ventured into Tibet. According to the later chronicles, the king of Tibet had been his devoted disciple, the queen his tantric consort. Long before the persecution of the dharma, Padmasambhava had departed Tibet for the Copper-colored Mountain, located on the isle of Lanka, where he lives today in his octagonal palace, called Lotus Light. But before doing so, he is said to have written, or dictated, thousands of texts on yellow paper in a coded script, and hidden them—inside pillars, in mountains, in lakes—all over Tibet. These were teachings, it is said, that the Tibetans would need at specific moments in the future; often the texts themselves contained a prophecy.

Thus, in the eleventh century, as the new sects of Tibetan Buddhism claimed authority by going to India to retrieve Indian texts, the ancient sect (or so it would be later designated) began to discover its own authoritative texts, Indian texts, or at least composed by an Indian master, without having to go to India; the texts had been concealed in the Tibetan landscape centuries before. Such texts were called *terma* (*gter ma*), "treasures." Many of the most influential instructions on death, the intermediate state, and rebirth belong to the genre of the treasure, including the work we know as *The Tibetan Book of the Dead*.

By the thirteenth century, bardo teachings had begun to proliferate widely in Tibet. A Kagyu text from the period enumerates fifteen separate lineages of bardo instructions.[2] All sects developed instructions and prayers in a genre called "liberation from the straits of the bardo" (*bar do 'phrang sgrol*), whose purpose was to "close the womb door"—that is, to put an end to rebirth, or at least prevent rebirth in an unfortunate realm.

But centuries before, at the court of King Trisong Detsen, Padmasambhava is said to have made a prophecy. He predicted that in the coming degenerate age, virtuous deeds will only provoke resentment, monks will break their vows of celibacy, and the world will descend into factionalism and strife. At this time of turmoil, special instructions will be necessary to prevent beings from falling into negative rebirths as animals, ghosts, and hell beings. Padmasambhava then declared:

> So to benefit the sentient beings of this
>   degenerate age,
> I have committed [this cycle of teachings] to
>   writing,
> And concealed them at Mount Gampodar.
> In that age, a supremely fortunate son will be
>   born.
> His father will have the name Accomplished
>   Master Nyinda,
> And he will be the courageous "Karma
>   Lingpa."
> On his right thigh there will be a mole,
> Resembling the eye of pristine cognition,

And he will be born in the dragon or snake
   year
Into a heroic family line, the fruit of past
   good actions.
May that fortunate person encounter this
   [teaching].

But he [Karma Lingpa] should not publicly
   teach the cycles of
The *Peaceful and Wrathful Deities: Natural
   Liberation through [Recognition of]
   Enlightened Intention*
To anyone at all, even by whispering into the
   wind,
And so it should remain until the time of the
   third lineage holder.
Obstacles will arise if these [teachings] are
   publicly taught.
However, he should impart the cycle of the
*Great Compassionate One: Lotus Peaceful and
   Wrathful Deities*
To all of his fortunate students.

If the oral instructions of the lineage issuing
   from the third generation lineage holder
Are kept secret for seven years, there will be
   no obstacles.

When seven years have passed,
That [third generation successor] may
    properly impart to others
The empowerments and practical application
    of the [abridged] cycle,
The *[Great] Liberation [by Hearing] during
    the Intermediate States*.
Then, when nine years have passed, the
    [complete] cycle of the
*Natural Liberation through [Recognition of]
    Enlightened Intention*
Should be imparted gradually, not all at once.

These treasures will be extracted in the region
    of Dakpo, in Southern Kongpo,
And they will be concentrated for the sake of
    living beings,
In the region of Draglong, in Upper Kongpo.
Karma Lingpa's activity on behalf of living
    beings will ripen in the north.[3]

As we shall see in what follows, everything in
Padmasambhava's prophecy uncannily came true.
Thus, in accordance with the prophecy, around 1350
a son was born to a treasure-revealer name Nyida
Sangye (Nyi zla sangs rgyas, Sun-Moon Buddha).
The child's name was Karma Lingpa (Karma gling

pa). At the age of fifteen, he engaged in the practices necessary for him to discover textual treasure himself. The revealers of treasure are regarded as the reincarnations of Padmasambhava's own disciples, students to whom he had personally bestowed tantric initiation. In order to find the treasure, it was said to be necessary for the reincarnated student to manifest the mind of clear light, the same state of mind that Padmasambhava had revealed to the previous incarnation, centuries before. The mind of clear light manifests at death, but it also manifests during orgasm. The discovery of treasure is therefore often preceded by the practice of sexual yoga with a consort. That consort, however, is also predestined for her partner, in some cases, named in a prophecy by Padmasambhava or his consort. But in the case of Karma Lingpa, something went wrong. He chose the wrong woman, who bore him a son.

Despite the apparent mismatch, Karma Lingpa successfully extracted two treasure texts from Gampodar (Sgam po gdar) Mountain, assisted by his father. The first was entitled *Peaceful and Wrathful Deities: Natural Liberation through [Recognition of] Enlightened Intention* (*Zhi khro dgongs pa rang grol*). The second was entitled the *Great Compassionate One, the Peaceful and Wrathful Lotus* (*Thugs rje chen po padma zhi khro*). He already had a circle of disciples, to whom he bestowed the teachings of the second text, while restricting the teachings of the first text to a single disciple. He is also said to have produced a digest of yogic teachings from the discovered texts, which he entitled *Instructions on the Six Bardos* (*Bar do drug khrid*).

But his failure to find the appropriate consort bore bitter fruit. According to one account, his consort ran away with his attendant, only to return with him to poison Karma Lingpa. Knowing that he was dying, Karma Lingpa attempted to save himself through the practice of consciousness transference (*grong 'jug*, literally "entering a corpse"), a practice at which his father was adept. Asking his father to watch over this body for three days, he caused his consciousness to enter the body of a dead bird. The bird then came back to life and flew to a distant mountain, where the antidote to the poison grew. Just as the bird was returning to Tibet on the third day, Karma Lingpa's evil attendant and his consort insisted that the body be cremated. The bird descended on Karma Lingpa's corpse and was about to deposit the healing fruit in his mouth, when it was attacked by the attendant. The bird flew away and the fruit burned in the flames, together with Karma Lingpa's body.

Among the many biographies of the great treasure revealers of the Nyingma sect, that of Karma Lingpa is one of the less glorious; his untimely death left much undone. His father and his son are said to have found among his possessions various manuscripts, some finished, some not, connected with the series of funeral rites that would come to be known as *Bardo Tödöl, Liberation in the Intermediate State through Hearing.* The task of consolidating the texts, as well as the treasures that he had discovered, seems to have fallen to Karma Lingpa's son, and to his son's disciple. They likely played a central role in the creation of the work that would eventually come to be known, through a series of transformations, as *The Tibetan Book of the Dead.*

It seems clear that those transformations began shortly after Karma Lingpa's death, through a process of revision and reorganization, by many hands, making it difficult to identify which parts derive from Karma Lingpa himself. However, from the various accounts and descriptions that have survived, some of which include references to works no longer extant, it would appear that the collection of works attributed to Karma Lingpa's discovery (known as the *Peaceful and Wrathful Deities*) was a set of texts—texts that foliated in the subsequent centuries—designed for dealing with the dead, specifically, for guiding the spirit of the deceased to the next lifetime, ideally to a happy rebirth, both for the sake of the dead and for the sake of the living, so that the surviving family may be free from the contagion (whether natural or supernatural) that had brought about the death.

The universe through which the dead would wander was composed of three bardos. The first, and briefest, is the bardo of the moment of death (*'chi kha'i bar do*) when the profound state of consciousness called the clear light dawns. If one is able to recognize the clear light as reality, one is immediately liberated from rebirth. If not, the second bardo begins, called the bardo of reality (*chos nyid bar do*, a term that seems to be a Nyingma innovation). The disintegration of the personality brought on by death reveals reality, but in this case, not as the clear light, but in the form of a *maṇḍala* of forty-two peaceful deities and a *maṇḍala* of fifty-eight wrathful deities. These deities appear in sequence to the consciousness of the deceased in the days immediately following death. If reality is not recognized in this second bardo, then the third bardo, the bardo of existence (*srid pa bar do*), dawns, during which one must again take rebirth in one of the six realms—that of gods, demigods, humans, animals, ghosts, or hell beings.

These texts provide instructions for the post-mortem confession and expiation of negative deeds and violated vows; for bestowing initiation; for reciting mantras; for making ritual cakes (*gtor ma*) and burnt offerings; for the making of amulets to be placed on the corpse, the so-called "liberation by wearing"; prayers to be recited by the officiating priest, both requesting assistance from the buddhas and bodhisattvas, and offering advice and comfort to the departed soul wandering in the bardo, especially in visualizing the one hundred peaceful and wrathful deities of the *maṇḍala* and avoiding rebirth in an unfortunate realm.

The instructions to the departed on the experience of the *maṇḍala* of peaceful deities on the second day after death provide an example of the style of the text. As described in the previous chapter, at the time of death, a series of dissolutions of the elements takes place; first earth, then water, then fire, then air. On the second day of the bardo, the water element appears in the purified form of white light. From that, in the east, the buddha called Vajrasattva will appear. He is blue in color, holding a five-pronged vajra in his right hand. He is seated on an elephant throne and is in sexual union with his consort, named Buddhalocanā. They are accompanied

by two male bodhisattvas and two female bodhisattvas. Here are the instructions to the spirit of the
departed person:

A [brilliant] white light, [indicative of] the
mirror-like pristine cognition, which is the
natural purity of the aggregate of form, white
and dazzling, radiant and clear [will emanate]
from the heart of Vajrasattva and his consort
and it will shine piercingly before you [at the
level of your heart, with such brilliance] that
your eyes cannot bear it. Together with this
light of pristine cognition, a dull smoky light,
[indicative of] the hell [realms], will also
dawn before you [and touch your heart]. At
that time, under the sway of aversion, you will
[wish to] turn away in fear and terror from
the bright white light and come to perceive
the dull smoky light of the hell [realms] with
delight. At that moment, you should fear-
lessly recognise the white light, white and
dazzling, radiant and clear, to be pristine cognition. Have confidence in it. Be drawn to it
with longing devotion. Pray with devotion,
thinking, "This is the light ray of the tran-
scendent lord Vajrasattva's compassion. I take
refuge in it." This, in reality, is Vajrasattva and

his consort come to escort you on the dangerous pathway of the intermediate state. This is
the light-ray hook of Vajrasattva's compassion. Be devoted to it. Do not delight in the
dull smoky light of the hell [realms]. This
[dull light] is the inviting path of the negative
obscurations created by your own deep aversion, which you yourself have generated. If
you become attached to it, you will fall into
the realms of hell, sinking into a swamp of un-
bearable suffering, from which there will be
no [immediate] opportunity for escape. [This
dull light] is an obstacle blocking the path to
liberation. Do not look at it. Abandon your
aversion. Do not be attached to it. Do not
cling to it. Be devoted to the white light, radiant, and dazzling.[4]

Similar instructions are provided for each of the
seven days of the bardo, as different visions, and different deities appear. Eventually added to the cycle
of texts were advanced instructions for master med-
itators on how to identify the most profound nature of reality, in preparation for their own deaths.

The story of Karma Lingpa and of the transmission of his treasure would not be told until 1499, a
century after Karma Lingpa's demise, when a monk

named Gyarawa (Rgya ra ba, born 1430) completed a work entitled *A Garland of Jewels*. He had received the transmission himself from one Nyida Özer (Nyi zla 'od zer), who had received them from Karma Lingpa's son. In the versions of the cycle of texts that have come down to the present day, Gyarawa is listed as author or editor of twenty-five works, almost all of which deal with mortuary ritual. He also is listed in five separate transmission lineages of the Karma Lingpa cycle. This suggests that Gyarawa performed two important roles in the history of what has come to be known as *The Tibetan Book of the Dead*. First, he took what had likely been a somewhat amorphous cycle of texts and organized them into a more coherent ritual system that performed a variety of funerary functions. Second, he used his position as a high-ranking monk—he occupied the throne of Menmo (Sman mo) monastery and seems to have founded as many as seven others—to disseminate the Karma Lingpa rituals to monastic institutions in southern Tibet, the primary sites for the performance of funerals in the region.[5] Gyarawa is likely "the third generation lineage holder" proclaimed by Padmasambhava in the prophecy cited here, thus providing a clue for the date of the prophecy's composition.

Yet despite the crucial editorial and institutional

efforts of Gyarawa, the work as we have it today would not assume its present form until the seventeenth century, through the efforts of one Rigzin Nyima Drakpa (Rig 'dzin nyi ma grags pa, 1647–1710), himself a treasure-revealer, whose previous incarnations would be said to include the star-crossed consort of Karma Lingpa.

He was born in the kingdom of Nang chen in eastern Tibet to a family with strong ties to the Kagyu sect. As a child, he was sent to a Kagyu monastery to study, but experienced a vision of Padmasambhava and eventually received permission from his father to receive instruction from a Nyingma lama. He would eventually study with many of the leading Nyingma teachers of the day, traveling extensively throughout Tibet and visiting Bhutan, Nepal, and India. He developed a reputation both as a revealer of treasures and a subduer of demons, attracting a large circle of influential patrons who made generous offerings for his services, including the regent of the fifth Dalai Lama. By the time he was thirty, he was widely regarded as a custodian of Karma Lingpa's revelations, well qualified to transmit its teachings. Around 1680 (and perhaps continuing until his death), Rigzin Nyima Drakpa began organizing and editing various transmissions associated with Karma Lingpa into a sequence of liturgies and prayers in seventeen chapters, entitled *Liberation in the Intermediate State through Hearing*, the *Bardo Tödöl*.

His achievement was to place seventeen smaller texts into a sequence for use in a funeral ritual, with individual works connected with the three standard stages of death, intermediate state, and rebirth. Thus, the work begins with instructions on how to recognize the mind of clear light at the moment of death and thereby achieve liberation. If this opportunity is missed, visions of a *maṇḍala* of forty-two peaceful deities appear, followed on the fourteenth day by a *maṇḍala* of fifty-eight wrathful deities. Prayers are provided, requesting assistance from the buddhas and bodhisattvas at this time, and instructing the deceased in how to navigate the straits of the bardo. The deceased then acquires a mental body and begins to make its way to the next rebirth. To aid it in finding a fortunate rebirth, prayers and mantras are provided for the purification of negative karma.

Rigzin Nyima Drakpa seems to have been something of a controversial figure, in part because of his skill in the black arts, providing individual patrons with the means to destroy their enemies and empowering local chieftains to repel invaders. It is possible that his fame in this regard contributed to the popularity of his edition of the *Bardo Tödöl*, which was first carved onto woodblocks and printed near the end of the eighteenth century. The *Bardo Tödöl* would eventually become but one of a variety of liturgies from which a local lama could draw in ministering to the spirits of the dead.

On March 20, 1888, British troops crossed the Sikkimese border into Tibet. Ten thousand Tibetan troops and militia were dispatched, fighting the British in battles around Mount Lungdo from June through October of that year. The thirteenth Dalai Lama Thupten Gyatso—twelve years old at the time—and his regent launched a campaign called "Repel the Foreign Army" (Phyi gling dmag zlog). Many Tibetans were killed in the fighting, and funeral rituals were performed for them.

The British invaded Tibet again in 1903. Tibetan militia resisted with swords, spears, and antique matchlock rifles, suffering several thousand dead in more than a dozen battles and skirmishes. But they were unable to stop the advance, and British troops under the command of Colonel Francis Younghusband marched into Lhasa on August 3, 1904. The Dalai Lama had already fled to Mongolia. A treaty was signed, according to which Tibet agreed to have relations with no foreign power other than Great Britain. More practically, the treaty allowed the British to establish trade missions in three Tibetan towns, (but not in the capital Lhasa), including the second largest city in Tibet, Gyantse. As a result, with the Tibetans' grudging assent, British officers would begin going back and forth between the British colony of India and Tibet. Fifteen years later, in 1919, one such officer, Major W. L. Campbell, bought a thick set of block prints of Tibetan mortuary texts in Gyantse. He brought these back to India, where he would sell them to an American who was on a kind of spiritual holiday to Asia. The result of this purchase would be yet another example of the strange things that can happen when Americans go abroad.

The World

From Egypt, Walter Evans-Wentz traveled to Sri Lanka and then on to India, where he visited the Theosophical Society headquarters at Adyar in Madras. He met Annie Besant, who had become president of the society after the death of Henry Steel Olcott in 1907. In the subsequent decade, Besant had turned the focus of the Theosophical Society away from Buddhism and toward Hinduism. From Madras, Evans-Wentz continued up the east coast of India to Puri in Orissa, where he studied with various Hindu gurus, including Swami Satyananda (1896–1971). In 1919, he arrived in Darjeeling in the Himalayas of West Bengal, a hill station established by the British East India Company in the previous century. In 1888, as a result of the first British invasion, a trade route between Tibet and India had been constructed through the district, and there was now a substantial Tibetan community in the area.

At the time of Evans-Wentz's visit to the Himalayas, the Victorian view of the history of Buddhism still dominated European scholarship. It regarded the Buddhism of the Buddha and his early followers as an ethical system that denied the existence of a creator deity and promoted the equality of man, rejecting the prejudice of caste and class. The Buddhism of the Buddha was a rational faith, free of all superstition and priestcraft. But after the Buddha's death, a period of degeneration began. With the rise of the Mahāyāna, all manner of deities, in the form of buddhas and bodhisattvas, were introduced in order to appeal to the masses, and Buddhist philosophy veered from the middle path into nihilism. The course of contamination continued with the rise of Buddhist tantra, which introduced debased Hindu practices, most notoriously, sexual yoga. The theme of degeneration was not unknown in Buddhist literature. Over the centuries, Buddhist texts had also decried the sad state of the dharma, but often with a promise of redemption in the form of a newly discovered teaching or in a prophecy of enlightenment under a future Buddha.

But for the Victorians, the history of Buddhism was one of relentless decline. A mere shadow of original Buddhism was belatedly transmitted to Tibet, where it was adulterated yet again, this time with the demon-worship of the Tibetans. As L. Austine Waddell, medical officer of the Younghusband expedition that invaded Tibet in 1903, wrote, "Lamaism is only thinly and imperfectly varnished over with Buddhist symbolism, beneath which the sinister growth of poly-demonist superstition darkly appears."[1] For Waddell, most Tibetan Buddhist practice was "contemptible mummery" and Tibetan Buddhist literature was "for the most part a dreary wilderness of words and antiquated rubbish, but the Lamas conceitedly believe that all knowledge is locked up in their musty classics, outside which nothing is worthy of serious notice."[2]

This view was widely held when Evans-Wentz arrived in India. Yet some also saw Tibet as a repository of lost wisdom, a wisdom of which the Tibetans themselves, apart from a secret brotherhood of initiates, were often ignorant. In 1894, Nicolas Notovitch published *The Unknown Life of Jesus Christ*, which included the translation of a manuscript the author claimed to have discovered in Ladakh. It was entitled "The Life of Saint Issa" and describes Jesus's activities during seventeen years in India and Nepal during the "Lost Years" that are unaccounted for in the Bible, from the time Jesus was twelve until the beginning of his ministry at age thirty. Jesus was also important to the Theosophists; the master Koot Hoomi had been Balthasar, one of the three Magi, in a previous incarnation. But the wisdom that Evans-Wentz sought extended far back before the time of Christ.

Evans-Wentz was a great collector of texts in languages that he never learned to read (he amassed a collection of Pāli palm leaf manuscripts while in Sri Lanka). Shortly after his arrival in Darjeeling, he bought some Tibetan texts from Major W. L. Campbell, a British army officer who had recently returned from Tibet. These were portions of the *Peaceful and Wrathful Deities: Natural Liberation through [Recognition of] Enlightened Intention* by Karma Lingpa. Provided with a letter of introduction from the local superintendent of police, Sardar Bahādur Ladenla[3] (with whom he would later collaborate on the final volume in his series), Evans-Wentz took these texts to Gangtok, the capital of Sikkim, and to the English teacher at its Bhutia Boarding School for boys: one Kazi Dawa Samdup (Ka dzi Zla ba bsam 'grub, 1868–1922).

Born in Sikkim in an ethnically Tibetan family, his younger brother went on to become a Theravāda monk known in Sri Lanka as Mahinda Thero, a famous poet and advocate of Sinhalese independence.

Kazi Dawa Samdup studied at the Bhutia Boarding School in Darjeeling, where his teacher was Sarat Chandra Das, a scholar and spy who was the model for the character of Hurree Chunder Mookerjee in Kipling's *Kim*. He excelled in English and was hired as an interpreter for the British Raj. While stationed in Bhutan from 1887–1893, he became the student and disciple of the Nyingma lama Tshampa Norbu (Mtshams pa nor bu). In 1905, the Maharaja of Sikkim appointed him as headmaster of the Bhutia Boarding School for boys in Gangtok, teaching English and Tibetan. He also served as the Maharaja's translator at events honoring the Prince of Wales in Calcutta in 1906 and the newly crowned George V in Delhi in 1911. In 1910, he acted as one of the interpreters for the thirteenth Dalai Lama's visit to India. In addition to these more ceremonial duties, he accompanied the British diplomat Sir Charles Bell (1870–1945) to the important Simla Convention in 1914, where British, Tibetan, and Chinese representatives attempted to establish the borders between China and Tibet and between Tibet and British India.[4]

By the time he met Evans-Wentz, Kazi Dawa Samdup was already acquainted with Western enthusiasts of Buddhism, having also served as translator for Alexandra David-Neel (who had received her Theosophical Society diploma in 1892). She described him in her most famous book, *Magic and Mystery in Tibet*:

> Dawasandup was an occultist and even, in a certain way, a mystic. He sought for secret intercourse with the Dâkinîs and the dreadful gods hoping to gain supernormal powers. Everything that concerned the mysterious world of beings generally invisible strongly attracted him, but the necessity of earning his living made it impossible for him to devote much time to his favourite study. . . .
>
> Drink, a failing frequent among his countrymen, had been the curse of his life. This increased his natural tendency to anger and led him, one day, within an ace of murder. I had some influence over him while I lived in Gangtok. I persuaded him to promise the total abstinence from fermented beverages that is enjoined on all Buddhists. But it needed more energy than he possessed to persevere. . . .
>
> I could tell many other amusing stories about my good interpreter, some quite amusing, in the style of Boccaccio. He played other parts than those of occultist, schoolmaster,

writer. But, peace to his memory. I do not wish to belittle him. Having acquired real erudition by persevering efforts, he was sympathetic and interesting. I congratulate myself on having met him and gratefully acknowledge my debt to him.[5]

Evans-Wentz took his texts to Kazi Dawa Samdup, and over the course of the next two months met with him each morning before the school day began. The translations that Kazi Dawa Samdup made for Evans-Wentz would eventually appear in three books: *The Tibetan Book of the Dead* (1927), *Tibetan Yoga and Secret Doctrines* (1935), and *The Tibetan Book of the Great Liberation* (1954).

Their time together was brief, with Evans-Wentz soon returning south to Swami Satyananda's seaside ashram in Puri to practice yoga, learning to sit motionless for four hours and forty minutes each day. Evans-Wentz studied with several of the prominent neo-Vedantin teachers of the day, including Satyananda's teacher, Sri Yuketswar, as well as Ramana Maharshi. He returned to Gangtok to visit Kazi Dawa Samdup in 1920, shortly before his appointment to the post of Lecturer in Tibetan at the University of Calcutta. This was to be their last meeting; Kazi Dawa Samdup died in 1922. In 1924,

Evans-Wentz visited Kazi Dawa Samdup's family in Kalimpong, from whom he received a manuscript translation of the *Rje btsun bka' 'bum* (*The Hundred Thousand Words of the Master*), which Evans-Wentz subsequently edited and published as *Tibet's Great Yogī Milarepa* (1928).

Evans-Wentz seems never to have been a devotee of Tibetan Buddhism. Of his relationship with Kazi Dawa Samdup, Evans-Wentz's biographer writes: "The few letters that have survived that they exchanged show a surprisingly distant and formal tone. Even in Dawa Samdup's diaries there is no word to suggest otherwise. There is nothing at all foreshadowing the later declarations that the Lama was the guru of Walter Evans-Wentz, nothing about the 'teachings' the American was supposed to have received."[6]

In 1935, after the publication of *The Tibetan Book of the Dead* and *Tibet's Great Yogī Milarepa*, Evans-Wentz returned to Darjeeling. He employed two Sikkimese monks to translate another work from the same cycle of texts as the *Bardo Tödöl*, entitled *Self Liberation through Naked Vision Recognizing Awareness* (*Rig pa ngo sprod gcer mthong rang grol*). During the same visit, he received a summary of a famous biography of Padmasambhava, prepared by Sardar Bahādur Ladenla, who had introduced him to Kazi Dawa Samdup some sixteen years before. These works would form the last work in the series, *The Tibetan Book of the Great Liberation*, eventually published in 1954.

Evans-Wentz returned to the United States in 1941, and spent the last twenty-three years of his life at the Keystone Hotel in San Diego. He spent his final months at the Self-Realization Fellowship of Swami Yogananda (a disciple of Sri Yuketsvar and author of the popular *Autobiography of a Yogi*) in Encinitas, California. Walter Evans-Wentz died in 1965.

Let us now turn finally to *The Tibetan Book of the Dead* itself, proceeding in order through the various prefaces and introductions.

The 1927 "Preface to the First Edition" of *The Tibetan Book of the Dead* must be read with Evans-Wentz's commitment to Theosophy in mind. He begins, "In this book I am seeking—so far as possible—to suppress my own views and to act simply as the mouthpiece of a Tibetan sage, of whom I was a recognized disciple." This is precisely the kind of claim that Madame Blavatsky so often made. He goes on to report that he has spent more than five years "wandering from the palm-wreathed shores of Ceylon, and thence through the wonder-land of the Hindus, to the glacier-clad heights of the Himalayan Ranges, seeking out the Wise Men of the

East." (xix) In his travels he had encountered philosophers and holy men who believed that there were parallels between their own beliefs and practices ("some preserved by oral tradition alone") and those of the Occident and, furthermore, that these parallels were the result of some historical connection. (xix)

In the 1948 "Preface to the Second Edition," he emphasizes what is a consistent theme in his annotations to the translation, that the West has largely lost its own tradition of the art of dying, well-known to the Egyptians, to the initiates of the "Mysteries of Antiquity," and to Christians of the Middle Ages and the Renaissance. This was a pre-Christian tradition (as he claims in his addendum to the translation, the Tibetan art of dying is a pre-Buddhist tradition) that had been wisely incorporated into the rituals of "various primitive Churches of Christendom, notably the Roman, Greek, Anglican, Syrian, Armenian, and Coptic," (xiv) traditions that have been ignored by modern medical science. A great hope shared by the late lama Kazi Dawa Samdup and other learned lamas, he says, was that their rendering of *The Tibetan Book of the Dead* would serve as a catalyst for the West to rediscover and begin again to practice an art of dying, finding the inner light of wisdom taught by the Buddha "and all the Supreme Guides of Humanity." (xvi–xvii) According to Theosophical doctrine, the Buddha was a member of the Eastern Hierarchy of Adepts.

By 1955 and the "Preface to the Third Edition," there is no further mention of the rediscovery of an Occidental tradition. Instead, "To each member of the One Human Family, now incarnate on the planet Earth, this book bears the greatest of all great messages. It reveals to the peoples of the Occident a science of death and rebirth such as only the peoples of the Orient have heretofore known." (vii) This was the edition in which the commentaries of Carl Jung and Lama Govinda were first incorporated, and his preface takes due notice of their insights. Beyond that, the references to Hindu works, especially the *Upanishads* and *Bhagavad Gītā*, already evident in the notes and various epigraphs scattered throughout the book, seem to outweigh the references to Buddhism and Tibet. Jung's commentary, he says, demonstrates that Western psychologists have moved beyond Freud; they will "advance much further when they no longer allow the Freudian fear of metaphysics to bar their entrance into the realm of the occult." (ix) He repeats the view found in much spiritualist and Theosophical literature of the nineteenth century: that Western science will eventually evolve to the point where it can confirm the insights of the East, most importantly, the existence of rebirth:[7]

> Thus it is of far-reaching historical importance that the profound doctrine of pre-existence and rebirth, which many of the most enlightened men in all known epochs have taught as being realizable, is now under investigation by our own scientists of the West. And some of these scientists seem to be approaching that place, on the path of scientific progress, where, as with respect also to other findings by the Sages of Asia long before the rise of Western Science, East and West appear to be destined to meet in mutual understanding. (ix)

It is when the current "heretical" psychologists adopt the methods of meditation and self-analysis taught by the master yogins that, "Western Science and Eastern Science will, at last, attain at-one-ment." (x) This leads him to a pronouncement worthy of Madame Blavatsky herself:

> Then, too, not only will Pythagoras and Plato and Plotinus, and the Gnostic Christians, and

Krishna and the Buddha be vindicated in their advocacy of the doctrine, but, equally, the Hierophants of the Ancient Mysteries of Egypt and Greece and Rome, and the Druids of the Celtic World. And Western man will awaken from that slumber of Ignorance which has been hypnotically induced by a mistaken Orthodoxy. He will greet with wide-opened eyes his long unheeded brethren, the Wise Men of the East. (x)

In his 1935 Psychological Commentary, C. G. Jung (who was well-read in the work of Madame Blavatsky's former secretary, G.R.S. Mead) states that *The Tibetan Book of the Dead* (which he refers to consistently as the *Bardo Thödol*) has been his constant companion ever since its publication in 1927 and "to it I owe not only many stimulating ideas and discoveries, but also many fundamental insights." (xxxvi) He thus sets for himself the modest task of making "the magnificent world of ideas and the problems contained in this treatise a little more intelligible to the Western mind." (xxxvi) He declares the Tibetan work to be psychological in its outlook, and begins to compare its insights to the more limited views of Freud. He makes extensive use of the three Tibetan terms used to describe the stages of death and rebirth. The first is *Chikhai Bardo* (*'chi kha'i bar do*), literally, the intermediate state of the moment of death, in which the various dissolutions that end in the dawning of clear light occur. The second is the *Chönyid Bardo* (*chos nyid bar do*), literally the intermediate state of reality, the actual period between death and the next rebirth during which the visions so vividly described in the text appear. The third is the *Sidpa Bardo* (*srid pa bar do*), literally, the intermediate state of existence, which occurs with the entry of the wandering consciousness into the womb, preceded by the witnessing of the primal scene of parental intercourse.

Jung argues that Freudian psychoanalysis, working backwards, has only been able to discover the last of the three bardos, the *Sidpa Bardo*, marked by infantile sexual fantasies. Some analysts claim even to have uncovered intrauterine memories. It is at this point that "Western reason reaches its limit, unfortunately." (xli) He expresses the wish that Freudian psychoanalysis could have continued even further, to the pre-uterine; "had it succeeded in this bold undertaking, it would surely have come out beyond the *Sidpa Bardo* and penetrated from behind into the lower reaches of the *Chönyid Bardo*" (xlii)—that is, Freud could have proven the existence of rebirth. Here, although he was unaware of the parallel, Jung is reminiscent of classical Buddhist proofs for the existence of rebirth, in which it is claimed that one moment of consciousness is produced by a former moment of consciousness, and that once it is conceded that consciousness at the moment of conception is the product of a previous moment of consciousness, rebirth has been proven. But more important for Jung is this opportunity to dismiss Freud before moving on to his own project. Some might judge this particular condemnation to be rather disingenuous, since Jung did not himself pursue the question of existence of rebirth (beyond the symbolic level) in the decades that followed.[8]

But the criticism of Freud is offered only in passing as Jung moves to his larger task, evident also in his other commentaries on Asian texts—that is, the incorporation of Asian wisdom into his own psychological theory. He begins with the suggestion that the Westerner read the *Bardo Tödöl* backwards, not from death to intermediate state to rebirth, but from rebirth back to intermediate state and then back to death—thus, *Sidpa Bardo*, followed by *Chönyid Bardo*, followed finally by *Chikhai Bardo*. The neurosis of the *Sidpa Bardo* has already been identified. The next step is to move on to the *Chönyid Bardo*, which is a state of "karmic illusion." (xliii) He takes this as an opportunity to interpret karma as psychic heredity, which leads very quickly to the archetypes of the collective unconscious. Of the archetypes to be mined from comparative religion and mythology, he writes, "The astonishing parallelism between these images and the ideas they serve to express has frequently given rise to the wildest migration theories, although it would have been far more natural to think of the remarkable similarity of the human psyche at all times and in all places." (xliv) Thus, apparently contra Evans-Wentz, Jung sees no historical influence between Asian yogins and the initiates of Greek mystery cults. They are instead primordial universal ideas within an omnipresent psychic structure. How else could one account for the fact that the very same idea, that the dead do not know that they are dead, is to be found in the *Bardo Tödöl*, American Spiritualism, and Swedenborg? (xliv–xlv)[9]

The horrific visions of the *Chönyid Bardo*, then, represent the effect of surrendering to fantasy and imagination, uninhibited by the conscious mind: "the *Chönyid* state is equivalent to a deliberately induced psychosis." (xlvi) Jung uses this as an opportunity to repeat a point that occurs in almost all of his writings about Asia: the great danger in Westerners' practicing yoga. The dismemberments that occur in the Buddhist hells described in the Tibetan text are symbolic of the psychic dissociation that leads to schizophrenia. (xlvii)

Thus, for Jung, a fundamental distinction between East and West is that in Christianity, initiation is a preparation for death, while in the *Bardo Tödöl*, initiation is a preparation for rebirth, preparing, "the soul for a descent into physical being." (xlix) This is why the European should reverse the sequence of the *Bardo Tödöl* such that one begins with the experience of the individual unconscious, moves then to the experience of the collective unconscious, and moving finally to the state in which illusions cease and "consciousness, weaned away from all form and from all attachment to objects, returns to the timeless, inchoate state." (xlviii–xlix) This sequence, he says, "offers a close parallel to the phenomenology of the European unconscious when it is undergoing an 'initiation process,' that is to say, when it is being analyzed." (xlix) He closes with the statement that "The world of gods and spirits is truly 'nothing but' the collective unconscious inside me." (li–lii)

Thus, Jung confidently reduces a complex religious system, with its own long tradition of commentary and exegesis, to his own psychological system: Initiation is psychoanalysis; gods and spirits are the collective unconscious. Jung wrote commentaries on a number of Asian texts: Evans-Wen-tz's *Tibetan Book of the Great Liberation*; Richard Wilhelm's translations of the *I Ching* and the Dao-ist alchemical text, *The Secret of the Golden Flower*; D. T. Suzuki's *Introduction to Zen Buddhism*, and others. Here, his comments on *The Tibetan Book of the Dead*, as well as his other writings, contain the same gross cultural stereotypes of East and West, the same admonitions that Europeans not practice yoga, the same unsuccessful attempt to interpret "Eastern" consciousness in light of his theory of the unconscious. A thorough study of Jung's misread-ing, willful and otherwise, of "Eastern Religions" remains to be written.

The next preface to the 1948 edition was by Lama Govinda, largely forgotten today, but one of the most influential figures in the representation of Tibetan Buddhism to the West in the first half of the twentieth century. Lama Anagarika Govinda had been born Ernst Lothar Hoffmann in Kassel, Germany in 1895.[10] He served at the Italian front during World War I, after which he continued his studies at Freiburg University in Switzerland. He became interested in Buddhism while living with expatriate European and American artists in Capri, publishing his first book, *The Basic Ideas of Bud-dhism and Its Relationship to Ideas of God* in 1920, a work that is apparently no longer extant. In 1928, ten years after Evans-Wentz had made the voyage, he sailed for Ceylon, where he studied meditation and Buddhist philosophy briefly with the Theravāda monk, Nyānatiloka Mahāthera (1878–1957). He was also German, born Anton Walter Florus Gueth in Wiesbaden. An accomplished violinist, he had been ordained in Rangoon in 1903. It was Nyānatiloka who gave Ernst Hoffmann the name Govinda. Govinda left Ceylon to travel in Burma and India. While visiting Darjeeling in 1931, he was driven by a spring snowstorm to a Tibetan monastery at Ghoom, where he met Tomo Geshe Rimpoche (Gro mo dge bshes rin po che), a Gelukpa lama. In his autobiographical *The Way of the White Clouds*, published over thirty years later, Govinda would depict their encounter and his subsequent initiation as a pivotal moment in his life. It is difficult to imagine what transpired between a Tibetan monk and a German traveler (dressed in the robes of a Theravāda monk, although he seems not to have been ordained) who spoke no Tibetan, or what this "initiation" may have been (it was perhaps the most preliminary of Buddhist rituals, the refuge ceremony); Govinda's description of any teachings he may have received are quite vague. However, he seems to have understood the term differently from its Tibetan meaning of an empowerment by a lama to engage in specific tantric rituals and meditations. In *Foundations of Tibetan Mysticism According to the Esoteric Teachings of the Great Mantra OM MAṆI PADME HŪṂ* he writes, "By 'initiates' I do not mean any organized group of men, but those individuals who, in virtue of their own sensitiveness, respond to the subtle vibrations of symbols which are presented to them either by tradition or intuition,"[11] a rather Theosophical gloss.

After making a pilgrimage to Mount Kailash in southwestern Tibet in 1932, he held brief teaching positions at the University of Patna and at Shantiniketan (founded by Rabindranath Tagore), publishing essays in *The Maha-Bodhi*, the journal of a Buddhist society in Calcutta, as well as various Theosophical journals. His lectures at Patna resulted in *The Psychological Attitude of Early Buddhist Philosophy* and his lectures at Shantiniketan resulted in *Psycho-Cosmic Symbolism of the Buddhist Stūpa*. While at Shantiniketan he met a Parsi woman, Rati Petit, whom he would marry in 1947. (She also assumed a new name, Li Gotami, and like her husband, dressed in Tibetan-style robes of his design.) During the 1930s, he founded a number of organizations, including the International Buddhist University Association, the International Buddhist Academy Association, and the Arya Maitreya Mandala. In 1942, he was interned by the British at Dehra Dun with other German nationals, including Heinrich Harrer (who would escape to spend seven years in Tibet) and the Theravāda monk Nyānaponika Mahāthera (1901–1994). He had been born Siegmund Feniger to a Jewish family in Hanau am Main, Germany. A distinguished Pāli scholar, he would become best known as the translator of Buddhaghosa's *Visuddhimagga*, which he rendered as *The Path of Purification*.

After the war, in 1947–1948, Lama Govinda and Li Gotami led an expedition sponsored by the *Illustrated Weekly of India* to photograph some of the temples of western Tibet, notably at Tsaparang and Tholing. (Li Gotami's photographs, which have important archival value since the Chinese invasion, appear in Govinda's *The Way of the White Clouds*, *Foundations of Tibetan Mysticism*, and her own *Tibet in Pictures*.) During their travels, they met a lama named Ajorepa Rimpoche at Tsecholing Monastery, who, according to Govinda, initiated them into the Kagyu order. No sect of Tibetan Buddhism has such an initiation ceremony; the nature of this ceremony also remains nebulous. As in the case of Tomo Geshe Rimpoche, Lama Govinda is mute on the teachings they received. Nonetheless, from this point on he described himself as an initiate of the Kagyu order, or as he often styled himself, "an Indian National of European descent and Buddhist faith belonging to a Tibetan Order and believing in the Brotherhood of Man."

Returning from Tibet, Lama Govinda and Li Gotami set up permanent residence in India, living in the Himalayan foothills in a house rented to them by Walter Evans-Wentz. During the 1960s, their home near the temple of Kasar Devi became an increasingly obligatory stop for spiritual seekers (including the Beat poets Gary Snyder and Allen Ginsberg in 1961) until they put up signs around the property warning visitors away. With the publication of *The Way of the White Clouds* in 1966, his fame only grew, and he spent the last two decades before his death in 1985 lecturing in Europe and the United States. His last years were spent in a home in Mill Valley provided by the San Francisco Zen Center. In 1981, Govinda published what he regarded as his most important work, *The Inner Structure of the I Ching*, a work that he undertook because, "We have heard what various Chinese and European philosophers and scholars thought about this book, instead of asking what the *I Ching* itself has to say."[12] His study seeks to remedy the situation, unimpeded and perhaps enhanced by his apparent inability to read Chinese. Like Jung, he commented freely on many forms of "Eastern Thought." The book was published through support from the Alan Watts Society for Comparative Research.

Indeed, throughout his career, Govinda seems to have drawn on a wide variety of Western-language sources, but never on untranslated Buddhist texts. In his book of essays, paintings, and poetry published by the Theosophical Society, *Creative Meditation and Multi-Dimensional Consciousness* (with such essays as "Concept and Actuality," "The Well of Life," and "Contemplative Zen Meditation and the Intellectual Attitude of Our Time"), the footnotes cite Martin Buber, D. T. Suzuki, Alan Watts, Heinrich Zimmer, and Walter Evans-Wentz. Nonetheless, he represents himself as a spokesman for Tibetan Buddhism in ways that are above all reminiscent of the Theosophy of Evans-Wentz:

> The importance of Tibetan tradition for our time and for the spiritual development of humanity lies in the fact that Tibet is the last living link that connects us with the civilizations of a distant past. The mystery-cults of Egypt, Mesopotamia and Greece, of Incas

and Mayas, have perished with the destruction of their civilizations and are forever lost to our knowledge, except for some scanty fragments.

The old civilizations of India and China, though well preserved in their ancient art and literature, and still glowing here and there under the ashes of modern thought, are buried and penetrated by so many strata of different cultural influences that it is difficult, if not impossible, to separate the various elements and to recognize their original nature.[13]

Just as Evans-Wentz portrayed himself as merely the mouthpiece of Kazi Dawa Samdup, so Lama Govinda suggests that his musings somehow derive from teachings he received from Tomo Geshe Rimpoche, to whom his *Foundations of Tibetan Mysticism According to the Esoteric Teachings of the Great Mantra OM MANI PADME HŪM* is dedicated, "The living example of this great teacher, from whose hands the author received his first initiation twenty-five years ago, was the deepest spiritual stimulus of his life and opened to him the gates to the mysteries of Tibet. It encouraged him, moreover, to pass on to others and to the world at large, whatever knowledge and experience he has thus gained—as far as this can be conveyed in words."[14]

The fact that this work provides an interpretation that appears in no Tibetan text may explain (as we shall also see in the case of Evans-Wentz) why he describes them as "esoteric teachings."

In his "Introductory Foreword," to *The Tibetan Book of the Dead*, Lama Govinda, like Jung, draws on a psychological vocabulary in stating that, "There are those who, in virtue of concentration and other *yogic* practices, are able to bring the subconscious into the realm of discriminative consciousness and, thereby, to draw upon the unrestricted treasury of subconscious memory, wherein are stored the records not only of our past lives but the records of the past of our race, the past of humanity, and of all pre-human forms of life, if not of the very consciousness that makes life possible in this universe." (liii) Govinda thus seems to combine Jung's notion of a collective and archaic repository of memory with Evans-Wentz's belief that *The Tibetan Book of the Dead* is drawn from the actual memories of Eastern yogins who had the ability to remember their past lives. However, such knowledge would crush those not trained to receive it, and thus the *Bardo Tödöl* has remained secret, "sealed with the seven seals of silence." Echoing Evans-Wentz's call, he declares, "But the time has come to break the seals of silence; for the human race has come to the juncture where it must decide whether to be content with the subjugation of the material world, or to strive after the conquest of the spiritual world, by subjugating selfish desires and transcending self-imposed limitations." (liv) The remainder of his foreword is taken up largely with a defense of the authenticity of the Tibetan *terma*, those texts hidden by Padmasambhava in the eighth century, and an argument for the purely Buddhist nature of the *Bardo Tödöl*, untainted by Bonpo influence. On this point, as we shall see, he appears to part company with Evans-Wentz.

The next foreword is by Sir John Woodroffe (1865–1936), a distinguished British jurist who served in a number of positions at the High Court of Calcutta, before being appointed Chief Justice in 1915. He was among the first Europeans to take a serious interest in Hindu tantra, publishing a number of works on the subject under the pseudonym, Arthur Avalon. His most famous work is *The Serpent Power: Secrets of Tantric and Shaktic Yoga*, published in 1919. Despite his editing of four books on Tibetan Buddhism, as we have seen, Evans-Wentz's allegiance was first to Theosophy and second to the Hinduism espoused by the neo-Vedantin swamis of the day. Tantra was regarded as the esoteric teaching of Hinduism and Woodroffe was its leading Anglophone proponent. This likely led Evans-Wentz to invite him to contribute to *The Tibetan Book of the Dead*. Unsurprisingly, Woodroffe persistently attempts to find in the Hindu, and in particular, the Hindu tantric literature to which he was so devoted, parallels, and ideally, precedents, for the doctrines set forth in *The Tibetan Book of the Dead*. He pauses to include an obligatory swipe at Tibetans for the way they mispronounce Sanskrit mantras. (lxxix)

Having finally made our way through the various prefaces, commentaries, and forewords, we come to Evans-Wentz's own lengthy introduction. It begins with a note explaining its function, a note worth quoting at some length:

The editor's task is to correlate and systematize and sometimes to expand the notes thus dictated, by incorporating such congenial matter, from widely separated sources, as in his judgement tends to make the exegesis more intelligible to the Occidental, for whom this part of the book is chiefly intended.

The translator felt, too, that without such safeguarding as this Introduction is intended to afford, the *Bardo Thödol* translation would be peculiarly liable to misinterpretation and consequent misuse, more especially by those who are inclined to be, for one reason or another, inimical to Buddhistic doctrines, or to the doctrines of a particular Sect of Northern Buddhism. He also realized how such an Introduction as is here presented might itself be subject to adverse criticism, perhaps on the ground that it appears to be the outcome of a philosophical eclecticism. However this may be, the editor can do no more than state here, as he has stated in other words in the Preface, that his aim, both herein and in the closely related annotations to the text itself, has been to present the psychology and teachings peculiar to and related to the *Bardo Thödol* as he has been taught them by qualified initiated exponents of them, who alone have the unquestioned right to explain them.

If it should be said by critics that the editor has expounded the *Bardo Thödol* doctrines from the standpoint of the Northern Buddhist who believes in them rather than from the standpoint of the Christian who perhaps would disbelieve at least some of them, the editor has no apology to offer; for he holds that there is no sound reason adducible why he should expound them in any other manner. Anthropology is concerned with things as they are; and the hope of all sincere researchers into comparative religion devoid of any religious bias ought always to be to accumulate such scientific data as will some day enable future generations of mankind to discover Truth itself—that Universal Truth in which all religions and all sects of all religions may ultimately recognize the Essence of Religion and the Catholicity of Faith. (1-2, note 1)

This remarkable note accomplishes many tasks. First, it locates the authority for the contents of the Introduction that is to follow not in Evans-Wentz but in the translator, who, significantly, Evans-Wentz consistently refers to as "the Lāma." It is the Tibetan lama's oral teachings that provide the basis of Evans-Wentz's words. Indeed, it raises the level of authority one step higher by invoking the power of lineage, stating that the exegesis derives from the lama's own guru, which was transmitted first to Kazi Dawa Samdup, and then from him to Evans-Wentz, in the tradition of guru to disciple. Evans-Wentz, then, has for the most part, as he states in his own "Preface to the First Edition," acted only as the mouthpiece of his lama, occasionally, "incorporating such congenial matter, from widely separated sources, as in his judgement tends to make the exegesis more intelligible to the Occidental, for whom this part of the book is chiefly intended." He reports that the late lama called him his "living English dictionary." (78) As we shall see, there will be much of such congenial matter, especially with regard to the theories of karma and rebirth, and with regard to "symbolism," matter that deviates significantly from the content of the *Bardo Tödöl*, but that is represented by this note as having the sanction of the lama and the lama's lama. For Evans-Wentz is claiming for himself the status of the initiate; he is setting forth the teachings "as he has been taught them by qualified initiated exponents of them, who alone have the unquestioned right to explain them." He thus vouchsafes that right for himself as the student of these masters, although whether his reference is to Tibetan lamas or mahatmas here is unclear.[15] At the same time, in the final paragraph, he professes as well the authority of the scholar, the anthropologist who is concerned with "things as they are," unconcerned with the articles of any particular faith. Thus, he claims for himself both the authority of Eastern religion (through his Tibetan lama) and Western science (through his Oxford degree). His task is the accumulation of scientific data, data that will one day lead all sects of all religions to see the Essence of Religion. One assumes that he means Theosophy.

Evans-Wentz begins the body of the Introduction by linking the *Bardo Tödöl* and *The Egyptian Book of the Dead*. The so-called *Egyptian Book of the Dead*, in Egyptian *rw nw prt m hrw* or "Utterances of Emergence during the Day," is a funerary text, containing a description of the afterlife and instructions on how to reach it, with prayers and spells to be pronounced during the post-mortem journey. A papyrus of the text was typically placed in the sarcophagus of the deceased. This practice extended for some three millennia, from the Old Kingdom to the Roman Period, with many variations to the text occurring over this period. With the European excavation of Egyptian tombs in the nineteenth century, dozens of papyri of the text were discovered, making it a subject of scholarly inquiry and popular interest well into the twentieth century. The text was dubbed the "Book of the Dead" (*Totenbuch*) by the Prussian Egyptologist and archaeologist Karl Richard Lepsius (1810–1884) in his 1842 publication, *Das Todtenbuch der Ägypter nach dem hieroglyphischen Papyrus in Turin mit einem Vorworte zum ersten Male Herausgegeben*.

Ancient Egypt and its mysteries had been particularly important to Madame Blavatsky; her first major work was entitled *Isis Unveiled*. Evans-Wentz had "begun my Tibetan researches fresh from three years of research in the ancient funeral lore of the Nile Valley" (22), although his information on *The Egyptian Book of the Dead* seems to derive from a series of lectures delivered at the British Museum by Helen Mary Tirard (1854–1943), published in London in 1910 as *The Book of the Dead* by the Society for Promoting Christian Knowledge. Evans-Wentz explains that as soon as he encountered the *Bardo Tödöl* in India, he recognized that, "As a mystic manual for guidance through the Otherworld of many illusions and realms, whose frontiers are death and birth, it resembles *The Egyptian Book of the Dead* sufficiently to suggest some ultimate cultural relationship between the two; although we only know with certainty that the germ of the teachings . . . has been preserved for us by a long succession of saints and seers in the God-protected Land of the Snowy Ranges, Tibet." (2) It was this "ultimate cultural relationship" that caused Evans-Wentz to dub his text, *The Tibetan Book of the Dead*.

He begins his introduction with a discussion of symbolism, claiming that "some of the more learned *lāmas*" have believed that "since very early times there has been a secret international symbol-code in common use among the initiates, which affords a key to the meaning of such occult doctrines as are all still jealously guarded by religious fraternities in India, as in Tibet, and in China, Mongolia, and Japan." (3) It is this supposed code that will allow him to make his most dubious deviations from what the Tibetan text states. Symbol-codes, he notes, are not unique to Buddhists, but have been used throughout the world, in Egyptian and Mexican hieroglyphics, by Plato and the Druids, by Jesus and the Buddha. In the case of the Buddha, his disciples have over the centuries, preserved teachings of his that were never written down, that form, "an extra-canonical, or esoteric, Buddhism." (5)

Throughout the Introduction, he makes reference to occult teachings known only to initiates of the esoteric tradition. Again, all of this takes on new meaning when read through the spectacles of Theosophy, where symbolism is of central importance. One quarter of the 1,500 pages of the 1888 edition of *The Secret Doctrine* is concerned with symbolism, of which Madame Blavatsky writes, "The study of the hidden meaning in every religious and profane legend, of whatsoever nation, large or small—pre-eminently the traditions of the East—has occupied the greater portion of the present writer's life."[16] It is therefore easy to see why Evans-Wentz would have sought the esoteric meaning in all that he read. In this pursuit he would even be encouraged by Tibetan lamas, at least the lamas that Madame Blavatsky claimed to know. In 1894, she published in *Lucifer* a letter she had received from one of the mahatmas, "Chohan-Lama of Rinch-cha-tze (Tibet) the Chief of the Archives-registrars of the secret Libraries of the Dalai and Ta-shü-hlumpo Lamas-Rimboche." In discussing the Tibetan canon, the Chohan-Lama explains (in a passage that is unimaginable for a Tibetan lama of the nineteenth century to have written):

> Could they even by chance have seen them, I can assure the theosophists that the contents of these volumes could never be understood by anyone who had not been given the key to their peculiar character, and to their hidden meaning.
>
> Every description of localities is figurative in our system; every name and word is purposely veiled; and a student, before he is given any further instruction, has to study the mode of deciphering, and then of comprehending and learning the equivalent secret term or synonym for nearly every word of our religious language. The Egyptian enchorial or hieratic system is child's play to the decipher-

ing of our sacred puzzles. Even in those volumes to which the masses have access, every sentence has a dual meaning, one intended for the unlearned, and the other for those who have received the key to the records.[17]

Evans-Wentz then launches into a discussion of the symbolism of the number seven, for the bardo lasts for a maximum of forty-nine days, seven times seven. The number also has symbolic meaning in Hinduism, in Hermetic writings, and in the Gospel of John. In nature, seven is important in the periodic table and in the "physics of color and sound." This proves that the *Bardo Tödöl* is "scientifically based."(7)[18] In his discussion of the esoteric meaning of the forty-nine days of the bardo, Evans-Wentz refers the reader to several passages from Madame Blavatsky's *The Secret Doctrine*, to which he adds, "The late Lāma Kazi Dawa-Samdup was of the opinion that, despite the adverse criticisms directed against H. P. Blavatsky's works, there is adequate internal evidence in them of their author's intimate acquaintance with the higher *lāmaistic* teachings, into which she claimed to have been initiated." (7, note 1) Later in the Introduction, he writes, "In other words, the *Bardo Thödol* seems to be based upon verifiable data of human physiological and psychological experiences; and it views the problem of the after-death state as being purely a psycho-physical problem; and is, therefore, in the main sci-entific." (34) His view, then, seems to be that the *Bardo Tödöl*, or at least its esoteric teachings, are most ancient, confirmed by the saints and seers of all the great civilizations of the past. The Judgment Scene, for example, has parallels in ancient Egypt, in Plato's *Republic*, and in "the originally pagan St. Patrick's Purgatory in Ireland." (37) At the same time, the esoteric teachings are also most modern, waiting to be confirmed by visionary scientists of the future. This is a conviction that later exponents of *The Tibetan Book of the Dead* would reprise in subsequent decades.

Evans-Wentz's most creative contribution to the Introduction to *The Tibetan Book of the Dead*, and the point least likely to have been endorsed by "the late Lāma Kazi Dawa-Samdup" and most espe-cially, by Dawa Samdup's teacher, is the interpreta-tion of the doctrine of rebirth.

As discussed in chapter 2 earlier, according to the classical Buddhist doctrine of rebirth, accepted in all the Buddhist cultures of Asia, since time im-memorial sentient beings have wandered through the six realms of rebirth, blown helplessly by the winds of karma. All beings have been gods, demigods, humans, animals, ghosts, and hell beings, migrating from one realm to another, up and down, in lifetime after lifetime, impelled by their own past deeds.

A very different theory of rebirth was put forward by Madame Blavatsky in *The Secret Doctrine*, the source of Evans-Wentz's view. There, claiming to be commenting upon the ancient *Book of Dzyan*, written in the secret language of Senzar, she explains that the universe is populated by individual souls, or monads, which are reincarnated according to the law of karma. All beings were once immaterial monads, until their fall into form. The goal of the long path of rebirth is to return to that original form through the cycles of evolution.[19] For humans, only rebirth as a human is possible; animals may reincarnate as higher species, but never vice versa.[20]

Thus, for Evans-Wentz, the traditional view that beings migrate up and down through the six realms of rebirth is only the exoteric teaching, the popular view intended for the masses; the esoteric doctrine is quite different. "In examining the Rebirth Doctrine, more particularly as it presents itself in our text, two interpretations must be taken into account: the literal or exoteric interpretation, which is the popular interpretation; and the symbolical or esoteric interpretation, which is held to be correct by the initiated few, who claim not scriptural authority or belief, but knowledge." (39–40) He concedes that the exoteric view "accepted universally by Buddhists, both of the Northern and Southern Schools—as by Hindus" is that consciousness can be embodied in a sub-human form in a lifetime after, even immediately after, embodiment as a human. This view is based on "the untested authority of *gurus* and priests who consider the literally interpreted written records to be infallible and who are not adept in *yoga*." (42) That "the brute principle of consciousness in its entirety and the human principle of consciousness in its entirety are capable of exchanging places with each other" is, for Evans-Wentz, an "obviously irrational belief." (59) Yet this, he concedes, is the view that the *Bardo Tödöl* conveys, when it is read literally.

The esoteric view, "on the authority of various philosophers, both Hindu and Buddhist, from whom the editor has received instruction" is quite different. The human form is the result of evolution, as is human consciousness. Thus, just as it is impossible for an animal or plant to devolve into one of its previous forms, so it is impossible for "a human life-flux to flow into the physical form of a dog, or fowl, or insect, or worm." (43) Thus, "man, the highest of the animal-beings, cannot become the lowest of the animal beings, no matter how heinous his sins." (43–44) The view that such retrogression could take place was regarded by the esotericists to be quite unscientific. (48) There can only be gradual progression and retrogression within a species. Only after ages of continual retrogression could it be possible for a human form to revert to the sub-human. Evans-Wentz claims that this was the view of the late lama, quoting him as referring to "a mere faded and incoherent reflex of the human mentality," a phrase difficult to imagine originating from a Tibetan lama, in English or Tibetan. What Evans-Wentz found particularly remarkable, however, was that the lama "expressed it while quite unaware of its similarity to the theory held esoterically by the Egyptian priests and exoterically by Herodotus, who, apparently, became their pupil in the monastic college of Heliopolis." (45)

Evans-Wentz appears to have held to his conviction that rebirth as an animal is impossible in Buddhism throughout his life, both before his encounter with the *Bardo Tödöl* and long after. We recall that in *The Fairy-Faith in Celtic Countries*, he had discussed the "Celtic esoteric theory of evolution," which was "a comprehensive theory of man's own evolution as a spiritual being both apart from and in a physical body, on his road to perfection which comes from knowing completely the earth-plane of existence."[21] And later, in his 1935 *Tibetan Yoga and Secret Doctrines* and his 1954 *The Tibetan Book of the Great Liberation*, he refers readers back to this exposition of the topic in *The Tibetan Book of the Dead*. In the commenting on an incident in the life of Padmasambhava in *The Tibetan Book of the Great Liberation* in which Padma Tsalag is reborn as a fly, he explains, "While the many, the exotericists, may accept this strange folk-tale literally, the more spiritually advanced of the Great *Guru's* devotees interpret it symbolically, as they do very much else in the Biography as a whole, the fly being to them significant of the undesirable characteristics of the unbridled sensuality associated with Padma Tsalag."[22]

But if this is the true teaching, why does the *Bardo Tödöl* appear to teach something different? "The *Bardo Thödol*, as a Doctrine of Death and Rebirth, seems to have existed at first unrecorded, like almost all sacred books now recorded in Pali, Sanskrit, or Tibetan, and was a growth of unknown centuries. Then by the time it had fully developed and been set down in writing no doubt it had lost something of its primitive purity. By its very nature and religious usage, the *Bardo Thödol* would have been very susceptible to the influence of the popular or exoteric view; and in our opinion it did fall under it, in such manner as to attempt the impossible, namely, the harmonizing of the two interpretations. Nevertheless, its original esotericism is still discernible and predominant." (54–55)[23] Thus, it seems that even the sacred teachings of the lamas, preserved for centuries in Tibet (Evans-Wentz argues, contra Govinda, that essentials of the text are pre-Buddhist in origin [73, 75], perhaps deriving from the Atlantean age), are subject to degeneration when the esoteric knowledge is committed to writing; the higher teaching of *Bardo Tödöl* is confused, perhaps, "because of corruptions of text." (58) But the true meaning is still accessible; if the "Buddhist and Hindu exotericists re-read their own Scriptures in light of the Science of Symbols their opposition to Esotericism would probably be given up." (57)[24]

For Evans-Wentz, the *Bardo Tödöl* is a reshaping of ancient teachings handed down orally over the centuries, recording the belief of countless generations concerning the post-mortem state. Once written down, corruptions inevitably crept into the text, such that it cannot be accurate in all details. Yet it remains scientific in its essentials. "In its broad outlines, however, it seems to convey a sublime truth, heretofore veiled to many students of religion, a philosophy as subtle as that of Plato, and a psychical science far in advance of that, still in its infancy, which forms the study of the Society for Psychical Research [which in 1885 had condemned Madame Blavatsky as a fraud]. And, as such it deserves the serious attention of the Western World, now awakening to a New Age, freed, in large measure, from the incrustations of medievalism, and eager to garner wisdom from all the Sacred Books of mankind, be they of one Faith or of another." (77–78)

He ends the book with the opinion that "the greater part of the symbolism nowadays regarded as being peculiarly Christian or Jewish seems to be due to the adaptations from Egyptian and Eastern religions. They suggest, too, that the thought-forms and thought-processes of Orient and of Occident are, fundamentally, much alike—that, despite differences of race and creed and of physical and social environment, the nations of mankind are, and have been since time immemorial, mentally and spiritually one." (241)

But what of the Tibetan text, the actually Tibetan component of *The Tibetan Book of the Dead*? In *The Tibetan Book of the Dead*, the various prefaces, commentaries, forewords, introductions, and addenda together constitute slightly less than twice the size of the translation of the Tibetan text itself.

But even this is misleading, since within the translation, Evans-Wentz's notes often take up at least half the page, in some cases up to 80 percent.

The translation encompasses seven chapters from the *Bardo Tödöl* cycle, organized by Evans-Wentz into Book I, Book II, and an Appendix. Book I deals with the "bardo of the moment of death" (*'chi kha'i bar do*) and includes instructions that are to be read to the dying person beginning from the point at which breathing is about to cease and the winds are beginning to enter the central channel. The instructions are intended to aid the dying person in recognizing the clear light that is about to dawn. If the clear light can be recognized at this point, liberation from rebirth can be attained.

Book I continues with perhaps the most famous section of Evans-Wentz's book, the description of the "bardo of reality" (*chos nyid bar do*) and the visions that occur in the intermediate state between death and rebirth. If the clear light is not recognized at the moment of death, the bardo of reality begins. The text describes a series of visions that take place over fourteen days: seven days of visions of peaceful deities and seven days of visions of wrathful deities. Over each of the first seven days, two lights appear. One light, a bright light, derives from a particular buddha or group of buddhas; the other light, a dull light, derives from one of the six places of rebirth. The dull lights appear in this order over the seven days: gods, hell beings, humans, ghosts, demigods, all six types of beings, and animals. In each case, the deceased is instructed not to be frightened by the dazzling lights of the buddhas—which lead to liberation—and not to be attracted to the dull lights of the various denizens of saṃsāra—which lead to rebirth. Over the next seven days, various blood-drinking wrathful deities appear. The text instructs the deceased to see these deities as manifestations of one's own mind. If one flees in fear, one will be reborn in saṃsāra.

The second section of the translation, Book II, deals with the last of the three bardos, the "bardo of existence" (*srid pa bar do*), at the end of which rebirth takes place. In order to navigate this realm successfully and avoid fear and confusion, the deceased, now a bardo being, receives a description of what it has become and the experiences it will have; for example, the deceased will see friends and relatives from its former life and will speak to them, but they will not reply. The bardo being is instructed to pray for the aid of the bodhisattva of compassion, Avalokiteśvara, in order to avoid rebirth in one of the lower realms. One will appear before the Lord of Death, who will count out one's good deeds with

CHAPTER 4

white pebbles and one's bad deeds with black pebbles. Yet throughout one should recognize that the entire horrifying scene is a hallucination and meditate on emptiness. Liberation is again possible at this moment, but if one becomes distracted, one will be reborn, with the place of rebirth determined by one's state of mind; if one is attached to one's past possessions, for example, one will be reborn as a ghost. The bardo being will now wander to various wombs; if it enters the womb it will not escape. Hence, the text offers five methods for closing "womb doors," methods such as meditating on one's tutelary deity and recalling one's past virtues. If it is not possible to avoid rebirth entirely, instructions are provided for selecting a good place of rebirth, such as Sukhāvatī, the pure land of Amitābha, the buddha of infinite light; or Tuṣita, the joyous heaven where the future buddha Maitreya resides. If one must enter a womb door, it should be the womb of a human, into a good family, powerful and virtuous. Book II ends with a statement of the efficacy of the instructions for bringing about liberation to the dead. The translation section of Evans-Wentz's text concludes with an appendix of four prayers to be read for the dead and learned by the living. These are followed by a brief colophon.

As noted in chapter 3, what is known in Tibet as

the *Bardo Tödöl* is not a single text, but rather a cycle of texts. The number of texts in the cycle varies; there are often between fifteen and twenty, which are in turn drawn from the much larger cycle of Karma Lingpa's *Peaceful and Wrathful Deities*. The block print of the text that Evans-Wentz purchased from Major Campbell had seventeen individual texts. Evans-Wentz also had in his possession three other texts. The first two were short sets of prayers, in two editions, which, according to Evans-Wentz, were not included in the block print. Finally, Kazi Dawa Samdup had his own manuscript of the text, which according to Evans-Wentz, corresponded to seven chapters of the block print, and included the prayers. Kazi Dawa Samdup seems to have translated the text from this manuscript, a text that has never been located or identified.

In his study of the history of the so-called *Tibetan Book of the Dead*, Bryan Cuevas has examined twenty-one editions of the Karma Lingpa cycle. Among the dozens of texts that occur, he identifies three as central to the performance of funeral rites. Of these, one is clearly the most important, appearing in twenty of the twenty-one extant editions. It is entitled *Liturgy for the Self-Liberation of Karmic Latencies* (*Chos spyod bag chags rang grol*). Evans-Wentz mentions the work in a footnote on page

193, mistranslating the title as "The Rite which Conferreth of Itself Liberation in [Virtue of] Propensity." But he does not translate the work that is most commonly read to the Tibetan dead. Instead, from the seventeen texts, seven were chosen for translation, consisting of three chapters of instruction and four prayers.

The three texts from the larger collection that Evans-Wentz selected for translation were the *Reminder of the Bardo of Reality* (*Chos nyid bar do'i gsal 'debs*, 83–131), the *Description of How the Wrathful Bardo Appears* (*Khro bo'i bar do 'char tshul bstan pa*, 131–51) and the *Identification of the Bardo of Becoming* (*Srid pa bar do'i ngo sprod*, 153–96). However, the tradition has generally regarded the first and third of these as meditation manuals to be employed by advanced tantric practitioners, rather than as mortuary instructions to be read to the ordinary dead; they are not part of a typical Tibetan funeral ritual. The irony, in the event that yet another was needed, is that Evans-Wentz selected two texts for the living and called them *The Tibetan Book of the Dead*.[25]

Thus, Evans-Wentz, at least from the perspective of their long history in Tibet, selected the wrong texts for translation, and then he dwarfed that translation with various introductions, forewords, commentaries, appendices, and footnotes. The translation became a code to be broken, using the cipher of another text that is somehow more authentic. For Evans-Wentz, the ur-text is Madame Blavatsky's *The Secret Doctrine*, itself her decoding of *The Stanzas of Dzyan* in the secret Senzar language, a work that she claimed to have received from the mahatmas in Tibet.

It seems, then, that Evans-Wentz knew what he would find in the Tibetan text before a single word was translated for him. It almost seems that Evans-Wentz's spiritual vacation could have taken him to any Asian country and that he could have randomly chosen any Asian text, and he would have produced some version of the book published in 1927. But he chose Tibet, and so the book is *The Tibetan Book of the Dead*. One must recall how important Tibet was for Theosophy as the secret abode of its imaginary mahatmas, sages who are not Tibetan, their very existence unknown to all but a few; the Tibetans, according to the Theosophists, practice a debased form of Buddhism. In James Hilton's 1933 novel, *Lost Horizon*, the inhabitants of the lamasery of Shangri-La are also not Tibetan; the happy Tibetans live far below, in the Valley of the Blue Moon.

But, also ironically, Evans-Wentz was, in his own way, also being traditional. For, as we recall, the Tibetan work called the *Bardo Tödöl* is a treasure text (*gter ma*) said to have been written long ago, in the eighth century, but intended for a future time. So it was hidden away, only to be discovered six centuries later. Even then, it was revealed to its discoverer in the secret *ḍākinī* language, a kind of code that only he was able to decipher and translate into a public language. It was necessary, then, for the discoverer, finding the text at the prophesied moment, to become a kind of embodied ghost writer, translating it in such a way as to make it meaningful for its time, creating a text whose originality is derived from the fact that it is a copy. And so the text has come back to life at various historical moments. For the Anglophone world, that moment was 1927. Tibetan treasure revealers typically have "Ling" as part of their name, as in Karma Lingpa. What a coincidence that Evans-Wentz's middle name was Yeeling.

Evans-Wentz died in 1965, just as *The Tibetan Book of the Dead* was reborn yet again for a new generation of readers. Almost four decades after its publication, *The Tibetan Book of the Dead* remained one of the few Tibetan texts available in English translation. It, or excerpts from it, was used in college classrooms, sometimes anthologized in collections of Buddhist scriptures and Asian texts. Along with the *Bhagavad Gītā* and the *Tao Te Ching*, it entered the canon of classics of Oriental mysticism for readers once again seeking the wisdom of the East.

In the late 1960s, Evans-Wentz's old book found yet another audience as a new fascination with death swept the United States. No longer simply an exemplar of Asian wisdom, it became a world spiritual classic. Between 1968 and 1972, some twelve hundred books were published on the topic of death and dying, approximately the same number that had been published on the same topic between 1935 and 1968, one of the deadliest periods in human history. Among these twelve hundred books, perhaps none was more famous than Elisabeth Kübler-Ross's 1969 *On Death and Dying*, a handbook for the dying and their loved ones. This was the first of many books that she would write on the subject. In her 1975 *Death: The Final Stage of Growth*, she offered high praise to Evans-Wentz's book, "the various Buddhist teachings concerning death and the most efficacious way of 'living toward death' are presented in a most imaginative manner in the book which is currently purchased by more people in the western world than any other work, with the possible exception of the Bible, namely, *The Tibetan Book of the Dead*."[26]

In the following year, Stackpole Books of Harrisburg, Pennsylvania published a small book by the parapsychologist Raymond Moody, entitled, *Life After Life: The Investigation of a Phenomenon— Survival of Bodily Death*. Moody's book, an unexpected bestseller that went on to spawn a genre, detailed what have come to be known as "near-death experiences." It recounts the experiences of persons considered clinically to be near or at the point of death, yet who have revived to describe such things as floating above their body, moving through a dark tunnel toward a bright light, and encountering beings of light, sometimes recognized by Christians as Jesus. In a chapter entitled "Parallels," Moody explains that the *Bardo Tödöl* was "compiled from the teachings of sages over many centuries in prehistoric Tibet and passed down through these early generations through word of mouth." After providing a brief summary of the bardo experiences, Moody concludes, "In short, even though the *Tibetan Book of the Dead* includes many later stages of death which none of my subjects have gone so far as to experience, it is quite obvious that there is a striking similarity between the account in this ancient manuscript and the events which have been related to me by twentieth-century Americans."[27]

Sparked perhaps by such praise, a new translation

appeared in 1975, by Francesca Fremantle and Chö-gyam Trungpa (1939–1987), a prominent incarnate lama of the Kagyu sect, whose excellent English and controversial style had made him a popular Buddhist teacher in Britain and the United States. Among his British students was David Bowie who sang, on his 1971 album *Hunky Dory*, "If I don't explain what you ought to know, you can tell me all about it on the next Bardo." Fremantle and Trungpa translated the same sections of the larger *Bardo Tödöl* that Evans-Wentz had chosen. Trungpa's commentary employs the vocabulary of depth psychology that was in fashion in the 1970s, noting that, "The animal realm is characterised by the absence of sense of humour."[28]

In 1992, the Tibetan lama Sogyal Rinpoche published *The Tibetan Book of Living and Dying*, where accounts of the deaths of ordinary people are interwoven with scenes of the passing of great masters, illustrated by quotations from Milarepa, Padmasambhava, and the current Dalai Lama. But Sogyal's points are also supported by citations of other masters. There are quotations from Montaigne, Blake, Rilke, Henry Ford, Voltaire, Origen, Shelley, Mozart, Balzac, Einstein, Rumi, Wordsworth, and the Venerable Bede, that, taken together, provide a cosmopolitan eclecticism to Sogyal's message.

Rather than European and American psychologists lauding *The Tibetan Book of the Dead*, in this work, a Tibetan lama cites Elisabeth Kübler-Ross and Raymond Moody approvingly. The book has sold over one million copies. In 1994, Robert Thurman published a translation of the same chapters as Evans-Wentz, plus three others, published again as *The Tibetan Book of the Dead*, in the Bantam Wisdom Edition series.[29] And in 2000, Stephen Hodge and Martin Boord published *The Illustrated Tibetan Book of the Dead*, an "abridged and simplified version," which contained a new translation of the same chapters, with a commentary and many photographs of Tibet.

In 2005, Penguin Books published a new translation. The front cover reads:

First Complete Translation
The Tibetan Book of the Dead
Introductory Commentary by His Holiness
the Dalai Lama
Hidden Away For Many Centuries
This Ancient Treasure Text Reveals
The Secrets Of Enlightened Living
And Life After Death

The back cover reads, "This exquisite masterpiece presents the Tibetan Buddhist vision of our journey to inner development and guides those who wish to think beyond the cycle of a conventional lifetime to achieve a vastly greater and grander state of being."

The term "complete translation" is difficult to define in the case of the *Bardo Tödöl*, which, as we have noted, is not so much the title of a text as the name for a cycle of texts, of which there are multiple editions with varied contents. In this new translation, the amount of translated material is more than double that in Evans-Wentz's text. Seven more texts from Nyima Drakpa's redaction are added, three other texts from *Peaceful and Wrathful Deities: Natural Liberation through [Recognition of] Enlightened Intention* that are not part of Nyima Drakpa's redaction are added, one standard prayer is omitted, and the order of the texts is changed in order to accord with "the meaningful sequence of the intermediate states that arise in the course of life and death."[30] Yet, regardless of whether it is "complete," the new translation is a vast improvement. Many more texts of the cycle are translated for the first time, the translation is made from a better manuscript, and the translation is more accurate than that first published in 1927.[31]

The other words on the front and back describe the Tibetan text as "an ancient treasure" "hidden away for many centuries," that "reveals the secrets of enlightened living and life after death" to take us "beyond the cycle of a conventional lifetime" to "a vastly greater and grander state of being." This language mixes the Tibetan metaphors of treasure texts hidden away by enlightened masters, with the language of the New Age, where ancient secrets are revealed to make modern life meaningful. The sufferings of the six realms of rebirth become "the cycle of a conventional lifetime," the exalted state of buddhahood becomes "a vastly greater and grander state of being." The once secret teachings of Buddhist tantra are made accessible for personal development and spiritual growth. The press release from Penguin explained, "One of the greatest works created by any culture and overwhelmingly the most influential of all Tibetan Buddhist texts in the West is *The Tibetan Book of the Dead*. To date, there have been a number of distinguished translations but, strangely, all of these have been partial abridgements. [. . .The book] embraces the concept of enlightened living and the importance of being open to the wonders of the human experience while, at the same time, thinking beyond this lifetime to a vastly greater and grander cycle. With the growing trend towards searching for a deeper spirituality *The Tibetan Book of the Dead* will be a welcome and timely arrival for all those wishing to explore this aspect of their lives." Tibetan Buddhism as self-help.

This tone is largely missing when one opens the book. The book begins with an introduction by the fourteenth Dalai Lama, who provides a clear and learned contextualization of the material that will follow, setting forth Buddhist views of the nature of person, of the process of death, and of the principles of the practice of Highest Yoga Tantra. Such background is essential for understanding the Tibetan text, yet no such introduction had been provided in any of the previous translations. And it is noteworthy that the Dalai Lama deftly alludes to the relative obscurity of the *Bardo Tödöl* in Tibet. He only mentions *The Tibetan Book of the Dead* once, and then, only in the penultimate paragraph, where he writes:

> A sense of uncertainty, and often fear, is a natural human feeling when thinking about the nature of death and the relationship between living and dying. It is perhaps not surprising therefore that the *Bar-do Thos-grol Chen-mo*, the *Tibetan Book of the Dead*, a treasure-text which focuses on this important subject, has become one of the best-known works of Tibetan literature in the West.[32]

His implication is that the *Bar do thos grol chen mo* was not one of the best-known works of Tibetan literature in Tibet. Indeed, even given the great advances in scholarship on, and the popularity of, Tibetan Buddhism since the 1920s, it seems unlikely that the *Bar do thos grol chen mo* would have been translated into English even once, much less five times, by the beginning of the twenty-first century, had Evans-Wentz not purchased it from Major Campbell in 1919.

But he did, and during the last decades of British and American colonialism, the Tibetan text of the *Bardo Tödöl* became a kind of colonial commodity, the raw material exported to the city of the colonizer, where it is manufactured into a product that is then sold back to the colonizer, at a high price. In this case, that price has included compelling Tibetan teachers, most recently the Dalai Lama himself, to comment on the text yet again because it is the most famous Tibetan work in the Western world.

Our fear of death is certainly one reason for its fame. But the *Bardo Tödöl* became *The Tibetan Book of the Dead* and went on to become (at least according to its press release) "one of the greatest works created by any culture" for other reasons as well.

When Evans-Wentz chose to name his work *The Ti-betan Book of the Dead*, he had in mind *The Egyptian Book of the Dead*, convinced that both derived from a single source of ancient wisdom. The Old English word *boc* is connected to the word for beech tree. It thus may have meant "beech wood tablet," the sup-posed medium on which the ancient Germanic al-phabets, the runes, were carved (Madame Blavatsky wrote at length about the runes and their symbol-ism). By *book*, Evans-Wentz did not simply mean printed pages bound together. He likely had some-thing more venerable in mind, *book* in the sense of sacred book, Bible, *biblia*, a Greek word that comes from *byblos*, the name for the Phoenician port from which the Greeks imported Egyptian papyrus. For Evans-Wentz, *The Tibetan Book of the Dead* was something ancient, something sacred. It was a scripture. But how does a book (in the common sense of the term) become a scripture?

The sacred books of the Hindu tradition are the Vedas, "the knowledge," a collection of texts that date from 1500–1000 BCE. But according to the tradition, this date is far too late. The Vedas are described in Sanskrit as *apauruṣeya*, a term that literally means "not deriving from persons." One might assume that this means that the Vedas are not of human origin, but are rather divine. But the term "person" here includes both humans and gods. The Vedas are uncreated and eternal. It is even misleading to call them texts; they have existed forever in the form of sound, only becoming known when they were heard by the ancient sages (*ṛṣi*) long ago. It is also misleading to call them books. The Vedas were preserved orally for centuries by priests trained in sophisticated mnemonics. They were not written down for more than a millennium, and only then as the root text for commentaries; sound remains the preferred medium.

The Buddha rejected the authority of the Vedas by claiming that they had authors. And over the long history of Buddhism in India, Buddhist logicians debated with Hindu logicians over the nature of sound. One of the first syllogisms that a young Tibetan monk will learn is "Sound is impermanent because of being produced." This seems so obvious as to hardly warrant expression. The sound of a gong is produced by striking it with a hammer and then fades away until the gong is struck again and another sound is produced. Few young monks who memorize this syllogism understand that it arises from Buddhist debates against Hindus. If sound is impermanent, the Vedas cannot be eternal, and the claim that they are therefore preexistent truth is proven false.

But in order for the Buddha to establish his own authority it was not enough that he challenge the authority of his opponents, the Brahmin priests with whom he competed for prestige and patron-age. It was not enough for him to claim that he had discovered a reality unknown to them, that he had found a truth that had never been known before.

We do not know what the Buddha told his monks about his own path to enlightenment. As noted in chapter 2, he wrote nothing, and nothing of what he said was committed to writing until some four centuries after his death. But the texts that scholars consider to be the oldest do not de-scribe the four famous chariot rides and the con-frontation with aging, sickness, death, and the pos-sibility of escaping them. Instead, the Buddha recounts, "While still young, a black-haired young man endowed with the blessing of youth, in the prime of life, though my mother and father wished otherwise and wept with tearful faces, I shaved off my hair and beard, put on the yellow robe, and went forth from the home life into homelessness."[1]

Yet as biographies of the Buddha began to appear in the centuries after his death, it was not so much the events of his life that were retold but the events of his past lives, and especially his encounters with the buddhas of the past. For Śākyamuni was not the first person to become a buddha. Other buddhas had preceded him. The numbers vary; some texts say there were three previous buddhas, some say there were six, some say there were twenty-four. In each case, however, Śākyamuni Buddha met each of them in a previous life, over the course of many trillions of years.

Each of those buddhas had understood the same truth. And they had each done the same things. According to the Tibetan tradition, twelve deeds are done by all buddhas: (1) they all descend from the Tuṣita heaven, (2) they all enter into their mother's womb, (3) they all take birth, (4) as young men they all gain proficiency in the arts, (5) as young men they all enjoy the company of consorts, (6) they all renounce the world, (7) they all practice asceticism for a period of time, (8) they all seek enlightenment in Bodhgayā, (9) they all achieve buddhahood, (10) they all turn the wheel of the dharma, (11) they all perform miracles, and (12) they all pass into final nirvāṇa. After their passing, their bodies are cremated and their relics are enshrined in stūpas. Their teachings, and their relics, remain in the world for a certain period of time, but eventually the relics disappear and the teachings are forgotten. Only then does another bodhisattva, who has been perfecting himself over the previous eons, achieve enlightenment under a tree in Bodhgayā, realizing precisely the same truth that the previous buddhas had realized before him. He then teaches the dharma, the same dharma that the previous buddhas had taught and that the world has once again forgotten, at its peril. And so the same truth is taught again and again across the eons. And what is that truth? One of his first disciples famously summarized the Buddha's teaching in this way: "Of those things that have causes, he set forth their causes, and he also set forth their cessation."

We see, then, that even though the Buddha taught that all is impermanent, that truth of impermanence is itself eternal, being discovered and then taught, by buddha after buddha in age after age. Although dismissing the claim that the Vedas are an eternal truth that only later was heard by the sages, the Buddhists have their own obsession with the past and its authority, as a series of buddhas stretches back into an infinite past, each awakening to the same truth.

This obsession with the past, and suspicion of the present, manifests itself in Tibetan Buddhism in the form of *terma*, the treasure texts. As discussed in chapter 3, with the second wave of Buddhism in Tibet, the so-called "later spreading of the dharma," Tibetans—some monks, some laymen—went to India to procure texts and tantric initiations and bring them back to Tibet. Others even brought Indian masters back with them; Atiśa arrived in 1042. Whether Tibetan aspirants went to India or Indian masters came to Tibet, direct contact with the Indian tradition was established, short circuiting the break in transmission caused by the dark age that followed the assassination of the evil king Lang Darma in 842. This transmission was oral. Although many texts were carried across the Himalayas and into Tibet, those with the books on their back also transported something intangible. Just as the Vedas could be traced back in time without beginning, the Tibetan pilgrims had heard the dharma from their teacher, who had heard it from his teacher, who had heard it from his teacher, going back to the primordial source, the Buddha himself.

But what about those who had continued to practice Buddhism during the dark age? Journeys to India were perilous, descending from the Himalayan peaks to the Bengal plain, arriving as a foreigner confronted with strange languages, poisonous snakes, and unknown foods. And the pilgrims required resources; accounts of their sojourns in India commonly express concerns about gathering enough gold to exchange for the precious dharma. Yet without direct contact with Indian masters, how could the authority of one's practice be proclaimed?

Rather than making the long and harrowing journey to India, or inviting an Indian teacher to Tibet, a different form of authority appeared in the form of *terma*, the treasure texts composed by the Indian master Padmasambhava more than two centuries earlier and buried in the ground. This was a different form of connection to the past. Instead of traveling to India in order to hear what had been heard, traveling across dangerous distances in space in order to go back to a primordial time, those who discovered the treasures remained in Tibet. Instead of traveling across the surface of the earth, they dug beneath it to unearth the teachings of a second Buddha. These were not texts that were already known in India, but teachings intended especially for Tibet and secreted beneath its soil. And these were not texts that were foreign in origin, requiring first the laborious study of Sanskrit, then the meticulous translation from an Indian script into Tibetan, then oral commentary to render them relevant to the present. They were instead teachings that Padmasambhava had given in Tibet, teachings that had been transcribed by a Tibetan queen; they were time-release revelations, designed for a particular place, Tibet, and for a particular time, the present. Padmasambhava had placed the treasure texts in rocks, at the bottom of lakes, inside pillars of ancient temples, and in the minds of disciples yet unborn. He would often include a prophecy in the text about the circumstances of its future discovery. And at the appropriate time, he would instruct a future disciple about where to find the text. The medium of that message was a dream. The texts were not written in Sanskrit, but rather in a secret code, the language of the *ḍākinīs*, tantric goddesses. To read this text, one did not need to study Sanskrit in Kathmandu, as did those who traveled to India to retrieve the dharma. With the revelation of the text to its prophesied revealer came the spontaneous ability to translate the coded language into Tibetan.

Hidden texts, and their discovery, were not a Tibetan innovation. They had their own venerable history in Indian Buddhism. The Mahāyāna sūtras did not appear, at least to common sight, until several centuries after the Buddha passed into nirvāṇa. According to some accounts, the Buddha felt that the world was not yet prepared to receive these profound teachings and thus entrusted them to the safekeeping of various deities. Thus, after setting forth the Perfection of Wisdom (*prajñāpāramitā*) sūtras on Vulture Peak, the Buddha entrusted the *Perfection of Wisdom in Eight Thousand Lines* (*Aṣṭasāhasrikāprajñāpāramitā*) to the king of the yakṣas (a kind of nature spirit) named Kubera. He entrusted the *Perfection of Wisdom in Eighteen Thousand Lines* (*Aṣṭādaśasāhasrikāprajñāpāramitā*) to the gods. He entrusted the *Perfection of Wisdom in Ten Thousand Lines* (*Daśasāhasrikāprajñāpāramitā*) to the demigods. And he entrusted the *Perfection of Wisdom in One Hundred Thousand Lines* (*Śatasāhasrikāprajñāpāramitā*) to the nāgas, serpentine creatures who kept it in a jeweled casket at the bottom of the sea. It was retrieved by Nāgārjuna, the great master of Madhyamaka philosophy and expositor of emptiness (*śūnyatā*). And to certify the authority of Nāgārjuna, the Buddha made a prophecy that in the future it would be Nāgārjuna who would explain the Mahāyāna to the world.

In this way, the Buddha, who had long ago passed into the nirvāṇa without remainder, was able to extend his authority into the future; first by secreting his teachings among various gods and demigods in order that they could be revealed in the realm of humans at the appropriate time, and second, by making prophecies that established the credibility of those, yet unborn, who someday would reveal them, making what he had taught long ago newly known, ushering in a renaissance.

One of the earliest uses of the word "authority" in English is from 1230, where it refers to a book that provides conclusive testimony. As we have seen in the case of Hinduism and Buddhism, the weight of authority derives in large part from its origin in the past, whether there is an author or not. For the present needs the past. The present is a degenerate age, unable to solve the problems that afflict it; the solution lies in the past. And so long ago the Buddha gave teachings for the future and hid them in a jeweled casket at the bottom of the sea. Long ago, Padmasambhava dictated teachings for the Tibetans of the future and buried the scrolls of yellow paper beneath their soil. Long ago, the angel Moroni inscribed *The Book of Mormon* on golden plates and buried them on the hill Cumorah.

Yet we know that the Buddha did not teach the

Mahāyāna sūtras; they began to appear four centuries after his death. We know that Padmasambhava did not compose the thousands of treasure texts that continued to be discovered into the twentieth century; assuming that he was a historical figure, his time in Tibet was brief. But in order for religions to survive into the future, they require deep truths, and so they project the present into the past. Their truths are deep because they provide the foundation for the present, they are deep because their origin is distant from the present time, they are deep because they remain below the surface. Such truths must be located at a certain depth, a certain remove in time or space. That depth may be measured in eons of time or in feet beneath the surface. To retrieve those truths, one must go back in time or one must dig down in space.

But the truths that are retrieved are never unambiguous, they are always historical, if one can only know their history. And thus sometimes the retrojected text gains the authority of canon; sometimes it remains the musings of an eccentric. The fate of the text rests not on its content, but on the degree to which the circumstances of its composition remain shrouded from the light of history. How much do we know about the time when the newly composed text was backdated? In the case of the Mahāyāna sūtras, we know very little. In the case of the Tibetan treasures, we know something. In the case of Joseph Smith, perhaps we know too much.

The story of Joseph Smith holds many elements in common with the founding of a great religion. There is a visitation from an angel; the revelation of scriptures—indeed, scriptures inscribed on tablets in an ancient language; there are believers and unbelievers; there are prophecies fulfilled. Yet for many there is also a dissonance, one that resounds in part from the place and the time. The story does not take place in a distant land and ancient time, but in upstate New York in 1827. Perhaps there is too much that is familiar.

In chapter 1, I recounted the events of Smith's early life, up to publication of the *Book of Mormon*, as they might be recorded in a sacred history. Here, I will recount some of those same events, and the events leading to his early death, providing more historical detail. For, unlike so many founders, Smith lived in a time from which much survives.

Smith was born and raised in the "Burned Over District" at the time of the Second Great Awakening, a place and time of religious ferment that saw a diminution of the denominations of the colonial period—the Anglicans and Congregationalists—

and the growth of the Baptists and Methodists. The period also saw the rise of a number of religious movements collectively categorized as "Restorationist," who called for a return to the original Christianity of Jesus and the apostles, a Christianity from which the established denominations had deviated as a result of the Great Apostasy, which the various movements dated to various moments in the early history of the Church. According to Mormon theology, the period of the Great Apostasy began after Jesus's ascent into heaven and continued until Joseph Smith's first vision in 1820 (although not reported until 1832) in which Smith saw God and Jesus in the woods (now known as the Sacred Grove) near the family farmhouse. Other Restorationist churches that arose during this time and that continue to the present include the Disciples of Christ and the Seventh-Day Adventists.

Smith's father was known to use a divining rod in an effort to find buried treasure. Prior to his discovery of the golden tablets buried in the hill Cumorah in 1823, Joseph Smith had supported himself as a "scryer," earning up to fourteen dollars a month to look into a crystal and see what could not be seen by the naked eye, most often lost objects or buried treasure. In Smith's case, he would put his "seer stone" into a white stovepipe hat, which he then put over his face. It was through his reputation for scrying that Smith met his future wife. In 1825, Smith was hired by Josiah Stowell and William Hale to aid them in finding buried Spanish treasure near Harmony, Pennsylvania, where he met Emma Hale, a relative of William Hale. In 1826, Smith was arrested on a misdemeanor charge in Bainbridge, New York; court records identify him as a "Glass Looker." Scholars would thus identify Smith's discovery and translation of the tablets as an instance of the "folk religion" (what was once called "magic") that characterized many of the movements that emerged during the Great Awakening in the mid-Atlantic states.

On April 6, 1830, Smith formally established the Church of Christ, based upon his translations and revelations. A small congregation developed in the neighboring towns, but local opposition forced Smith and his followers to move to Kirtland, Ohio in the following year. In Kirtland in 1836, the Mormon leadership sought to establish a bank. When their request for a bank charter was denied by the Ohio state legislature, they formed the Kirtland Safety Society Anti-Banking Company on January 2, 1837, with Joseph Smith as cashier. It quickly failed, along with hundreds of state-chartered and private banks during the Panic of 1837, leaving debts of approximately $100,000. The failure of the bank, and Smith's role in it, led to great vexation within the Mormon community, with many leaving the church and others being excommunicated.

Joseph Smith next moved the congregation to Far West, Missouri, which he declared the New Zion. Part of his motivation for moving from Ohio to Missouri was to avoid the group of armed men seeking to arrest him on the charge of illegal banking. Yet dissent within the church and the often violent opposition from neighboring communities caused Smith to move once again, this time to Illinois, where the church purchased land in Hancock County and established a town that Smith called Nauvoo.

A number of Smith's supporters became disaffected during this period, due in part to rumors of his practice of polygamy or "plural marriage," something that he publicly denounced throughout his life. But his scribe reported that in 1843, the year before his death, Smith received a revelation in which Jesus commanded the practice and threatened damnation to all who condemned it. The historical origins of the practice are difficult to trace; some historians speculate that it may derive from Jacob Cochran, a number of whose Maine followers joined Smith's church in 1832. Cochran had preached the doctrine of "spiritual wifery," according to which each man could have seven wives. (Cochran was convicted of lewd and lascivious behavior and spent four years in prison.) Regardless of when Joseph Smith received his revelation, his promiscuity can be traced to at least 1831, when he narrowly avoided castration by a mob after it became known that he had had intercourse with the sixteen-year-old daughter of a family with whom Smith and his wife were living as boarders. Smith would marry many other women until the time of his death, often in secret ceremonies that sealed the union for eternity. Estimates range (not counting Emma Smith) from twenty-seven to eighty-four, although the higher numbers include many who were married or "sealed" to Smith after his death.

A church newspaper, the *Nauvoo Expositor* published its one and only issue on June 7, 1844. It denounced Smith, saying that he had fallen from his status as a true prophet through his profession of such doctrines as polygamy. Smith and the city council responded by declaring the newspaper to be a public nuisance and ordering that its printing press be destroyed. He was eventually charged with libel for the destruction of the *Nauvoo Expositor*. While awaiting trial in Carthage, Illinois, Joseph Smith was shot to death on June 27, 1844.

James Strang, another discoverer of ancient plates, also met an untimely death. He declared himself the rightful and chosen successor of Joseph Smith, and produced a letter of appointment from Smith, designating Strang as his heir. The letter carried a Nauvoo, Illinois postmark of June 19, 1844, just a week before Smith's death. In further support of his destiny, the following year he discovered his own set of plates, the *Record of the Rajah Manchou of Vorito*. His translation of them revealed a prophecy that read, "The forerunner men shall kill, but a mighty prophet there shall dwell. I will be his strength, and he shall bring forth thy record." This, together with the letter, seemed to support his position as prophet. Yet his claim was rejected, leading him to form a rival church called the Church of Christ of Latter Day Saints (Strangite). He attracted a large number of supporters, over two thousand of whom moved with him to Beaver Island in Lake Michigan in 1848. Strang assumed both ecclesiastical and temporal leadership of his church, and was crowned king in a ceremony on the island on July 8, 1850. He was elected to the Michigan House of Representatives and wrote a highly regarded natural history of Beaver Island. He was assassinated in 1857.

On October 21, 1888, forty years after the first

rappings were heard in her family farmhouse in Hydesville, New York, Margaret Fox appeared on the stage of the New York Academy of Music to confess that she and her sisters had not been in contact with the spirits of the dead. The rappings had been produced by a skillful cracking of the joints of their hands and feet. An article published that day in the *New York World* entitled, "Spiritualism Exposed: Margaret Fox Kane Confesses Fraud," declared:

> But the severest blow that Spiritualism has ever received is delivered to-day through the solemn declarations of the greatest medium of the world that it is all a fraud, a deception, a lie. This statement is made by Mrs. Margaret Fox Kane, who has been able, through long training and early muscular development, to produce peculiar rappings and knocks which were affirmed to be spiritual manifestations, and which were so skillfully done as to baffle all attempts at discovery.

The article continued, "As the first and greatest of all mediums the weight of their evidence can not fail to sound the death knell of the abominable business which they, at an age when they knew not what they did, began and have seen flourish into one gigantic world-wide fraud."

In 1882, the Society for Psychical Research was founded in London by a group of prominent British spiritualists and scientists. Its purpose was to carry out scientific investigations of paranormal phenomena. In 1884, it conducted an investigation of Madame Blavatsky. One of its researchers, Richard Hodgson, was sent to India, where he examined many of the letters received from the mahatmas. The report issued by the society found:

> That there is consequently a very strong general presumption that all the marvellous narratives put forward as evidence of the existence and occult power of the Mahatmas are to be explained as due either (a) to deliberate deception carried out by or at the instigation of Madame Blavatsky, or (b) to spontaneous illusion, or hallucination, or unconscious misrepresentation or invention on the part of the witnesses.[2]

The report concluded, "For our own part, we regard her neither as the mouthpiece of hidden seers, nor as a mere vulgar adventuress; we think that she has achieved a title to permanent remembrance as one of the most accomplished, ingenious, and interesting imposters in history."[3]

Those who sought to dispense ancient wisdom on American soil in the nineteenth century suffered a variety of fates; some were murdered, some were simply denounced. Although Joseph Smith's followers went on to establish what some regard as the most American of Christian denominations, his own legacy remains controversial. Madame Blavatsky, who inspired many of the greatest poets and painters of the turn of the century, is but vaguely remembered a century later.

This is not to suggest a direct lineage from Joseph Smith, to the Fox sisters, to Madame Blavatsky, to Evans-Wentz. Joseph Smith was not a spiritualist, in the sense of someone who communicates with the spirits of the dead, as the Fox sisters and Madame Blavatsky claimed to do. Yet they all belong to a larger lineage, the lineage that Catherine Albanese has called American Metaphysical Religion. Here, Smith was but one of many visionaries, visionaries like Mary Baker Eddy, founder of the Church of Christ, Scientist, and Ellen White, a founder of the Sabbatarian Adventists. But one of the things that sets Smith apart from these other founders is that his vision bore a physical form; he dug it from the earth in upstate New York. It is this element of Smith's revelation that connects him, in one of the uncanny parallels so beloved by Evans-Wentz, to *The Tibetan Book of the Dead*. For this Latter Day Saint was also a latter day treasure discoverer (*gter ston* in Tibetan), a latter day Karma Lingpa for America. Like Karma Lingpa, he unearthed texts from the soil of his native land. Like Karma Lingpa, he died an early and violent death. Like Karma Lingpa, he left a long and complicated legacy. But Joseph Smith's teachings (as well as those of Madame Blavatsky) have been discredited, at least by some, regardless of their importance. And they have been discredited not for reasons of intrinsic value, regardless of how that might be measured, but, at least in part, because they lived in a chronologically recent and geographically proximate past.

But what of Walter Wentz? His *Tibetan Book of the Dead* has mystified and inspired readers around the world for almost a century. When Tibetan Buddhism was little known or understood, his was a groundbreaking work, the first to bring the translation of Tibetan Buddhist texts to the English-speaking public. Evans-Wentz was equally avant-garde in his method, collaborating with a Tibetan scholar, a practice that would not become common for another four decades, after the Tibetan diaspora that began in 1959. And unlike so many scholars of the colonial period, Evans-Wentz does not hesitate to credit his collaborator, going so far as to include his name in the extended title of the book.

But Evans-Wentz was another kind of colonizer. Just as the mahatmas had colonized a secret region of Tibet, so Evans-Wentz colonized a Tibetan text, turning it into a tome of his American version of Theosophy. Indeed, there is a certain audacity about the book; Evans-Wentz thought that he understood what he read, reading, as he did, through the lenses of Theosophy and Hindu Yoga. What is particularly troubling in his case is that, in an effort to add authority to his beliefs, he seemed compelled to represent his own eccentric interpretation of the Tibetan text as originating not from him, but from his Tibetan teacher. Evans-Wentz duly acknowledges the crucial role of Kazi Dawa Samdup in the creation of *The Tibetan Book of the Dead*. Yet he also exploits that collaboration in an effort to represent his own Theosophical reading as somehow authentic, attributing to the Tibetan, after his death, a position that he almost certainly did not hold. In Dawa Samdup's silence, Evans-Wentz speaks in the Tibetan's voice, in a language he never learned.

So, donning the Urim and Thummim of the

scholar, we see that Walter Wentz did something wrong. His crime was to pretend that his text originated from a time and place, where in fact it did not. And he got away with it. Evans-Wentz did not receive the condemnation suffered by Madame Blavatsky and the Fox sisters and Joseph Smith, because he did not claim that his authority derived from himself or his automatic writing, it did not derive from his ability to contact the dead or to converse with angels. It came, he claimed, from an ancient text unearthed in faraway Tibet. That is, Evans-Wentz fabricated his lineage, claiming that his strange views were those of "his lāma." In so doing, he was able to derive authority for himself by projecting it back to a distant and largely unknowable past. If we were to trace the lineage of *The Tibetan Book of the Dead*, it would not be Walter Evans-Wentz back to Kazi Dawa Samdup to Karma Lingpa to Padmasambhava. It would be Walter Evans-Wentz to Helena Petrovna Blavatsky to Colonel Olcott to the Fox sisters. Evans-Wentz took American Metaphysical Religion and gave it a Tibetan Buddhist pedigree.

But the fabrication of lineage is what, from the perspective of historical scholarship, Tibetans had done for centuries. The fabrication of lineage is what, from the perspective of historical scholarship,

Joseph Smith had done. In each case, the bodily resurrection of texts from native soil provides a connection to a sacred past. America is no longer
merely the destination of immigrants whose scriptures came from a distant Holy Land; sacred scriptures of the Christian faith are buried in American
soil; Carthage, Illinois is a place where martyrs
died; Kirtland, Ohio is a place of pilgrimage. Tibet
is no longer the distant borderland beyond the
Snowy Range, dismissed as a "yak pen" by Indian
abbots. Sacred Buddhist texts are buried there.

In the cycle of texts called the *Bardo Tödöl* unearthed by Karma Lingpa, Padmasambhava—the
enlightened master who came from India to Tibet—
makes prophecies about Tibetan lamas yet unborn,
prophecies that came true. And Joseph Smith found
these words of Lehi—the Israelite prophet who led
his family from Jerusalem to America—inscribed
on the buried plates, "But, said he, notwithstanding
our afflictions, we have obtained a land of promise,
a land which is choice above all other lands; a land
which the Lord God hath covenanted with me
should be a land for the inheritance of my seed. Yea,
the Lord hath covenanted this land unto me, and to
my children forever, and also all those who should
be led out of other countries by the hand of the
Lord." (*Book of Mormon*, 2 Nephi 1:5)

Tibet became a place of prophecy, and its fulfill-
ment, as did America. And all because something
was buried beneath a mountain—whether it be
Mount Tambora in Indonesia, Mount Gambodar
in Tibet, or the hill Cumorah in upstate New York.

Sometime between 1817 and 1821, Antonio Lebolo, a former soldier in Napoleon's army, excavated mummies from the necropolis of Thebes. Eleven of those mummies (and their accompanying papyri) were shipped to Trieste and then eventually to New York, where they were purchased by Michael H. Chandler in 1833. Chandler put together a traveling exhibition that toured the eastern United States, selling seven of the mummies in the process. In July 1835, he brought the four remaining mummies and some rolls of papyri to Kirtland, Ohio, having apparently heard of Joseph Smith's skills as a translator of ancient documents in Reformed Egyptian. Smith and his associates purchased the four mummies and at least five papyri for the large sum of $2,400. Smith then undertook the translation of the texts. His translation indicated that one of the texts was the *Book of Abraham*, a work in five chapters by Abraham himself, in which he describes his early life and how an angel of God saved him from being sacrificed by Chaldean priests, and his journey from Ur to Canaan and then to Egypt. Abraham describes how he observed the sun, the moon, and the stars using the Urim and Thummim. The final two chapters contain a description of God's creation of the earth and its creatures, concluding with Adam's naming of the animals.

Smith's translation was not published until 1842, after he had moved to Nauvoo, Illinois, where it appeared in three installments in the church's periodical *Time and Seasons* with the title *A Translation of some ancient Records, that have fallen into our hands from the catacombs of Egypt.—The writings of Abraham while he was in Egypt, called the Book of Abraham, written by his own hand, upon papyrus*. The translation was accompanied by facsimiles of three of the drawings from the papyri.

After Joseph Smith's death, the papyri were assumed to have been lost, perhaps when the Chicago Museum burned in the Great Chicago Fire of 1871. However, at least a portion of Smith's papyri collection, including the works from which the *Book of Abraham* was translated, was discovered in the Metropolitan Museum of Art in New York in 1966.

They had been pasted onto a piece of heavy paper, on the back of which was a map of Kirtland, Ohio and plans for a temple. The three illustrations revealed significant lacunae, which had been filled in, apparently at Smith's instruction, by the artists who had drawn the three facsimiles. When compared against other funerary papyri, it was clear that significant liberties had been taken. What should have been the soul of Osiris, a winged creature with a human head, had been given the head of a bird and identified by Smith as an angel of God. The god Anubis, a human figure with the head of a jackal, was given a human head and identified as a priest of Elkenah holding a knife, about to sacrifice Abraham. The papyri themselves were dated by Egyptologists as coming from the late Ptolemaic or early Roman periods. Rather than coming from Abraham, they were in fact fragments of two texts commonly used in Egyptian funerals. One text was *The Book of Breathing* (also known as *The Breathing Permit of Hor*). The other text was *The Egyptian Book of the Dead*.

INTRODUCTION

1. Sigmund Freud, *The Standard Edition of the Complete Psychological Works of Sigmund Freud*, vol. 14 (London: Hogarth Press, 1957), p. 289.

2. The Tibetan language has many silent letters which, when rendered in transliteration, make words largely unpronounceable for those who do not read Tibetan. For example, the name of the fourteenth Dalai Lama in transliteration is Bstan 'dzin rgya mtsho, which is pronounced something like *den zin gya tso*. The title of our text in transliteration is *Bar do thos grol*, which is pronounced something like *par doe tur drul*; the *th* in *thos* indicates an aspirate *t*, rather than the *th* sound of English. In this book, I will use the phonetic rendering *Bardo Tödöl* for the title of the text. In *The Tibetan Book of the Dead*, Evans-Wentz calls it the *Bardo Thodöl*.

3. The seven are the five translations of Evans-Wentz,

Francesca Freemantle and Chögyam Trungpa, Robert Thurman, Stephen Hodge and Martin Boord, and Gyurme Dorje, plus *The Psychedelic Experience* by Timothy Leary, Ralph Metzner, and Richard Alpert, and *The Tibetan Book of Living and Dying* by Sogyal Rinpoche. Related works include *Death, Intermediate State, and Rebirth in Tibetan Buddhism* by Lati Rinpochay and Jeffrey Hopkins (Ithaca: Snow Lion Publications, 1985), *Bardo Teachings* by Lama Lodo (Ithaca: Snow Lion Publications, 1987), *Secret Doctrines of the Tibetan Books of the Dead* by Detlef Ingo Lauf (Boston: Shambhala, 1977), and *Death and Dying: The Tibetan Tradition* by Glenn H. Mullin (Ithaca: Snow Lion, 1986). Mention should also be made of a substantial French translation, by Philippe Cornu, *Le livre des morts tibétain: La grande libération par l'écoute dans les états intermediaires* (Paris: Buchet-Chastel, 2009).

4. The first of these three was Sardar Bahādur S. W. Ladenla (1876–1936), a Sikkimese police officer from Darjeeling, who served the British in the Younghusband expedition. He later was hired by the government of the thirteenth Dalai Lama to establish a police force in Lhasa. He attended the Simla Convention in 1914 and later was personal assistant to Sir Charles Bell on his mission to Lhasa in 1921. On Ladenla, see Melvyn C. Goldstein's *A History of Modern Tibet, 1913–1951: The Demise of the*

Lamaist State (Berkeley CA: University of California Press, 1989), pp. 121–25, 159 and (for a rather more glowing portrayal), Evans-Wentz, *The Tibetan Book of the Great Liberation* (London; Oxford University Press, 1971), pp. 86–89. The other two translators were Geluk monks, Karma Sumdhon Paul and Lobzang Mingyur Dorje of Ghoom Monastery in Sikkim. They were both disciples of the Mongolian monk, Sherab Gyatso, the abbot of Ghoom. It was Sherab Gyatso who was the true author of Sarat Chandra Das's *Tibetan–English Dictionary*, a fact only acknowledged on the Tibetan title page of the work (my thanks to Dan Martin for pointing this out to me). On the lives of the two monks, see Evans-Wentz, pp. 89–92.

5. W. Y. Evans-Wentz, *The Tibetan Book of the Dead; or, The After-Death Experiences on the* Bardo *Plane, according to Lāma Kazi Dawa-Samdup's English Rendering* (London: Oxford University Press, 1960), p. xix. All subsequent references will be provided in the body of the text by page numbers in parentheses following the citation.

CHAPTER 1 America

1. The account of the life of Joseph Smith, both here and in the Conclusion and the Coda, is drawn largely from the compelling biography of Smith by Richard Lyman Bushman, *Joseph Smith: Rough*

Stone Rolling (New York: Vintage Books, 2007). For a fascinating survey of American "metaphysical" movements, see Catherine Albanese, *A Republic of the Mind and Spirit: A Cultural History of American Metaphysical Religion* (New Haven, CT: Yale University Press, 2007). Chapters 3–6 are especially pertinent to the figures discussed here.

2. http://www.strangite.org/Plates.htm.

3. Alfred Percy Sinnett, *Esoteric Buddhism* (London: Chapman and Hall, Ltd., 1885), pp. 181–82.

4. The influence of Theosophy on the study of Buddhism in Europe and America remains a largely unexplored topic. For a useful history of the Theosophical Society, see Bruce F. Campbell, *Ancient Wisdom Received* (Berkeley: University of California Press, 1980). For a biography of Henry Steel Olcott, see Stephen Prothero, *The White Buddhist: The Asian Odyssey of Henry Steel Olcott* (Bloomington, Indiana: Indiana University Press, 1996). Links between Theosophists and Tibetan Buddhism also merit a book-length study. For some preliminary comments, see Donald S. Lopez, Jr., *Prisoners of Shangri-La: Tibetan Buddhism and the West* (Chicago: University of Chicago Press, 1998), pp. 234–36.

5. In the "Cyclops" chapter of *Ulysses*, Joyce provides a parody of a Theosophical séance, and Madame Blavatsky's use and abuse of Sanskrit:

In the darkness spirit hands were felt to flutter and when prayer by tantras had been directed to the proper quarter a faint but increasing luminosity of ruby light became gradually visible, the apparition of the etheric double being particularly lifelike owing to the discharge of jivic rays from the crown of the head and face. Communication was effected through the pituitary body and also by means of the orangefiery and scarlet rays emanating from the sacral region and solar plexus. Questioned by his earthname as to his whereabouts in the heavenworld he stated that he was now on the path of prālāyā or return but was still submitted to trial at the hands of certain bloodthirsty entities on the lower astral levels. In reply to a question as to his first sensations in the great divide beyond he stated that previously he had seen as in a glass darkly but that those who had passed over had summit possibilities of atmic development opened up to them. Interrogated as to whether life there resembled our experience in the flesh he stated that he had heard from more favoured beings now in the spirit that their abodes were equipped with every modern home comfort such as tālāfānā, ālāvātār, hātākāldā, wātāklāsāt and that the

highest adepts were steeped in waves of vo-
lupcy of the very purest nature. Having requested a quart of buttermilk this was
brought and evidently afforded relief. Asked
if he had any message for the living he ex-
horted all who were still at the wrong side of
Māyā to acknowledge the true path for it was
reported in devanic circles that Mars and Ju-
piter were out for mischief on the eastern
angle where the ram has power. It was then
queried whether there were any special desires on the part of the defunct and the reply
was: *We greet you, friends of earth, who are still
in the body. Mind C.K. doesn't pile it on.* It was
ascertained that the reference was to Mr Cor-
nelius Kelleher, manager of Messrs H. J.
O'Neill's popular funeral establishment, a
personal friend of the defunct, who had been
responsible for the carrying out of the inter-
ment arrangements. Before departing he requested that it should be told to his dear son
Patsy that the other boot which he had been
looking for was at present under the com-
mode in the return room and that the pair
should be sent to Cullen's to be soled only as
the heels were still good. He stated that this
had greatly perturbed his peace of mind in
the other region and earnestly requested that
his desire should be made known.

> Assurances were given that the matter
> would be attended to and it was intimated
> that this had given satisfaction.

See James Joyce, *Ulysses* (New York: Modern Library, 1961), pp. 301–2.

6. W. Y. Evans-Wentz, *The Fairy-Faith in Celtic Countries* (New Hyde Park, NY: University Books, Inc., 1966), p. 140.

7. Ibid., p. 365. Later in the work, in note 1 on page 515, he observes that Darwin never identified exactly what it is that evolves, which cannot be something merely physical, since the physical dissolves at death. "Darwin thus overlooked the essential factor in his whole doctrine; while the Druids and other ancients, wiser than we have been willing to admit, seem not only to have anticipated Darwin by thousands of years, but also to have surpassed him in setting up their doctrine of re-birth, which explains both the physical and psychical evolution of man."

8. Ibid., p. 365.

9. Ibid., p. 490.

10. Ibid., pp. 377–78, note 2.

11. Ibid., p. 514.

CHAPTER 3 Tibet

1. Adapted from Erik Haarh, *The Yarlung Dynasty* (Copenhagen: G.E.C. Gad's Forlag, 1969), p. 144.

2. See Bryan J. Cuevas, *The Hidden History of the Ti-*

betan Book of the Dead (Oxford: Oxford University Press, 2003), p. 46.

3. See Gyurme Dorje, trans., *The Tibetan Book of the Dead* (London: Penguin Books, 2005), pp. xlii–xliii. For a similar prophecy, see Cuevas, pp. 87–88.

4. Gyurme Dorje, trans., *The Tibetan Book of the Dead*, pp. 238–39.

5. See Cuevas, pp. 128–31.

CHAPTER 4 The World

1. L. Austine Waddell, *The Buddhism of Tibet or La-maism*, cited from the 1972 Dover reprint issued under the new title, *Tibetan Buddhism: With Its Mystic Cults, Symbolism and Mythology* (New York: Dover Publications, 1972), p. xi.

2. Waddell, *The Buddhism of Tibet or Lamaism*, p. 157. Earlier in the book, Waddell had grudgingly conceded that "the Lāmas have the keys to unlock the meaning of much of Buddha's doctrine, which has been almost inaccessible to Europeans" (p. 17). Evans-Wentz knew Waddell's book; he cites this sentence approvingly on pages 2 and 3. However, he seems to have missed Waddell's dig at the Theosophists in his 1905 *Lhasa and Its Mysteries*. We recall that the Theosophists claimed Tibet to be the ethereal dwelling place of the telepathic mahatmas, preservers of Atlantean wisdom for the post-diluvian age. When Waddell finally was able to reach Lhasa,

as a member of the Younghusband expedition, he made it a point during his audience with the dGa' ldan Khri pa, who was left as head-of-state to negotiate with the British after the Dalai Lama had fled to Mongolia, of asking whether he had ever heard of the mahatmas. "Regarding the so-called 'Mahatmas,' it was important to elicit the fact that this Cardinal, one of the most learned and profound scholars in Tibet, was, like the other learned Lamas I have interrogated on the subject, entirely ignorant of any such beings." See L. Austine Waddell, *Lhasa and Its Mysteries: With a Record of the British Tibetan Expedition of 1903–1904* (New York: Dover Publications, 1988), pp. 409–10.

3. See note 4 in the Introduction.

4. See Dasho P. W. Samdup, "A Brief Biography of Kazi Dawa Samdup (1868–1922)," *Bulletin of Tibetology* 44 (no. 1 and 2) 2008, pp. 155–58.

5. Alexandra David-Neel, *Magic and Mystery in Tibet* (New York: Dover Publications, 1971), pp. 15, 17, 19.

6. Ken Winkler, *Pilgrim of the Clear Light* (Berkeley, CA: Dawnfire Books, 1982), p. 44. The other biographical information on Evans-Wentz in this chapter is drawn from Winkler's book. A useful summary is provided by John Myrdhin Reynolds in *Self-Liberation Through Seeing with Naked Awareness* (Barrytown, NY: Station Hill Press, 1989), pp. 71–78.

7. For a history of the claim that Buddhism and sci-

ence are compatible, see Donald S. Lopez, Jr., *Buddhism and Science: A Guide for the Perplexed* (Chicago: The University of Chicago Press, 2008).

8. Jung also sees fit to criticize Freud in his other preface for Evans-Wentz, his "Psychological Commentary" to *The Tibetan Book of the Great Liberation*, written in 1939. There, Jung claims that Freud's negative valuation of introversion is something that he shares with National Socialism. This is a shocking comment to make in 1939. Freud, who died in London that year at the age of 83, had fled from the Gestapo in Vienna in 1938. See W. Y. Evans-Wentz, *The Tibetan Book of the Great Liberation* (Oxford: Oxford University Press, 1954), p. xxxv.

9. On Jung's relation to Spiritualism and Theosophy, see Richard Noll, *The Jung Cult* (Princeton, NJ: Princeton University Press, 1994). Despite his apparent respect for Tibetan Buddhism, Jung refused to sign a letter protesting the Chinese invasion of Tibet in 1959. See Frank McLynn, *Carl Gustav Jung* (London: Bantam Press, 1996), p. 516.

10. The biographical details that follow are drawn from the rather reverential biography by Ken Winkler, *A Thousand Journeys: The Biography of Lama Anagarika Govinda* (Longmead, England: Element Books, 1990).

11. Lama Anagarika Govinda, *Foundations of Tibetan Mysticism* (New York: Samuel Weiser, 1969), p. 25.

12. Lama Anagarika Govinda, *The Inner Structure of the*

I Ching, The Book of Transformations (New York: Weatherhill, 1981), p. xi.

13. Lama Anagarika Govinda, *Foundations of Tibetan Mysticism* (New York; Samuel Weiser, 1969), p. 13.

14. Ibid., p. 14.

15. In his introduction to *Tibet's Great Yogī Milarepa*, there is a less ambivalent statement, "As from mighty broadcasting stations, dynamically charged with thought-forces, the Great Ones broadcast over the Earth that Vital Spirituality which alone makes human evolution possible; as the Sun sustains the physical man, They sustain the psychic man, and make possible mankind's escape from the Net of Sangsāric Existence." See W. Y. Evans-Wentz, *Tibet's Great Yogī Milarepa* (London: Oxford University Press, 1969), p. 18.

16. H. P. Blavatsky, *The Secret Doctrine*, vol. 1 (Los Angeles: The Theosophy Company, 1947), p. 303. This is a facsimile of the original 1888 edition.

17. "Tibetan Teachings" in H. P. Blavatsky, *Collected Writings 1883–1884–1885*, vol. 6 (Los Angeles: Blavatsky Writings Publication Fund, 1954), p. 98.

18. For the early Theosophists, "science" was often used as a synonym of "theosophy." See, for example, Henry Steel Olcott, *A Buddhist Catechism*, forty-fourth edition (Adyar, Madras: The Theosophical Publishing House, 1947).

19. H. P. Blavatsky, *The Secret Doctrine*, vol. 2, p. 303.

20. Ibid., p. 196 footnote. Madame Blavatsky was influ-

enced by the anthropology of the day, which saw the primitive peoples of the world as remnants of earlier ages of human evolution. She thus explains that those who evolve from the animal stage first take human form as what the *Stanzas of Dzyan* call "the narrow-brained," which includes South-Sea Islanders, Africans, and Australians. See *The Secret Doctrine*, vol. 2, p. 168.

21. W. Y. Evans-Wentz, *The Fairy-Faith in Celtic Countries*, p. 365.

22. W. Y. Evans-Wentz, *The Tibetan Book of the Great Liberation* (London: Oxford University Press, 1968), p. 116, note 1.

23. In his Introductory Foreword, Lama Govinda argues that the book is "not merely a mass for the dead, to which the *Bardo Thödol* was reduced in later times." (lxi)

24. Evans-Wentz reminds the reader that as early as 1911, in his *The Fairy-Faith in the Celtic Countries*, he had argued that the ancient Druid theory of rebirth provided "a scientific extension and correction" of Darwin's theory of evolution. He was thus gratified to find support for the theory of human reincarnation among such eminent scientists as T. H. Huxley, E. B. Tylor, and William James. (x, 60–61)

25. See Bryan J. Cuevas, *The Hidden History of the Tibetan Book of the Dead*, pp. 117–18. For a very useful description of the available manuscripts and printed versions of the Tibetan text, see pp. 205–15.

26, Elisabeth Kübler-Ross, *Death: The Final Stage of Growth* (New York: Touchstone Books, 1986), p. 69.

27. Raymond Moody, *Life After Life: The investigation of a phenomenon--survival of bodily death* (Harrisburg, Pennsylvania; Stackpole Books, 1976), p. 109.

28. See Francesca Freemantle and Chögyam Trungpa, trans., *The Tibetan Book of the Dead: The Great Liberation through Hearing in the Bardo* (Boulder, CO: Shambhala, 1975), p. 8. For a further discussion of this translation, see Donald S. Lopez, Jr., *Prisoners of Shangri-La*, pp. 76–78.

29. Thurman's translation includes the seven chapters translated by both Kazi Dawa Samdup and by Freemantle and Trungpa, and also adds three other texts from the Nyima Drakpa redaction of the *Bar do thos grol*. For a discussion of the Thurman and Sogyal volumes, see Donald S. Lopez, Jr. *Prisoners of Shangri-La*, pp. 78–85.

30. See Gyurme Dorje, trans., *The Tibetan Book of the Dead*, p. xlviii. The added texts are the *Gsang sngags rdo rje theg pa'i chos spyod thun bzhi'i rnal 'byor sems nyid rang grol* (which occurs at pp. 5–22 in the translation) and the *Rdzogs rim bar do drug gi khrid yig spyi don bzhi pa 'pho ba dran pa rang grol 'chi kha bar do'i gdams ngag* (which occurs at pp. 197–216 in the translation). The prayer that is omitted is the lineage prayer, *Brgyud pa'i gsol 'debs nges don rang grol.*

31. It should be noted, however, that the least problem-

atic element of Evans-Wentz's text is the translation. Kazi Dawa Samdup was a skilled translator, whose renderings were anachronized by Evans-Wentz's insistence on "thou," "hadst," and "wilt." For readers interested in comparing the original Evans-Wentz version to the 2005 "complete translation," pages 85–196 in Evans-Wentz correspond to pp. 225–303 in the 2005 translation. Evans-Wentz, pp. 197–98 correspond to 2005, pp. 308–9; Evans-Wentz, pp. 199–202 correspond to 2005, pp. 310–13; Evans-Wentz, pp. 202–5 correspond to 2005, pp. 32–34; and Evans-Wentz, pp. 205–8 correspond to 2005, pp. 314–16.

32. Gyurme Dorje, trans., *The Tibetan Book of the Dead*, p. xxvi.

CONCLUSION

1. See Bhikkhu Ñānamoli, trans., *The Middle Length Sayings of the Buddha* (Boston: Wisdom Publications, 1995), p. 256.

2. "Report of the Committee Appointed to Investigate Phenomena Connected with the Theosophical Society," *Proceedings of the Society for Psychical Research*, vol. 3 (December 1885), pp. 204–5.

3. Ibid., p. 207.

Abraham, 154
Albanese, Catherine, 147
Alpert, Richard, 9, 158
Amitābha, 115
Atiśa, 53, 133
Avalokiteśvara, 114
Avalon, Arthur. *See* Wood-
    roffe, John

Beatles, the, 9
Besant, Annie, 21, 71
Blavatsky, Helena Petro-
    vna, 19–23, 79, 82–83,
    101, 103–105, 107, 112,
    118, 128, 146–148, 150,
    167
Bowie, David, 122
Buddha, the, 30–31, 33–
    35, 43–47, 51, 72, 80,
    83, 103, 129–134,
    136–137

Campbell, W. L., 70, 74,
    116, 127
Chandler, Michael H., 153
Chögyam Trungpa, 122,
    158
Cohen, Leonard, 10
Coltrane, John, 9
Conan Doyle, Arthur, 8
Cuevas, Bryan, 116

Dalai Lama: Fourteenth,
    126–127; Thirteenth,
    69, 75, 158, 165
Darwin, Charles, 163, 168
David-Neel, Alexandra, 75

Eddy, Mary Baker, 147
Evans-Wentz, Walter Y.,
    2–7, 10–11, 21–26, 28–
    29, 71–75, 77–79, 92–
    97, 99–103, 105–

Evans-Wentz (*cont.*)
109, 111, 113, 115–120,
122–124, 127–128,
147–150

Fox, Margaret, 145
Fox Sisters, 18, 21–22, 147,
150
Freud, Sigmund, 1, 3, 7, 8,
81, 83–85, 157, 166

Gere, Richard, 10
Ginsberg, Allen, 92
Govinda, Lama Ana-
garika, 5, 81, 88–89, 91–
95, 111
Gyarawa (Rgya ra ba),
66–67

Harris, William, 16
Hilton, James, 118

James, William, 23, 168
Jung, Carl, 5, 81, 83–88, 93,
95, 166

Karma Lingpa (Karma
gling pa), 57–61, 65–67,
116, 148, 151
Kazi Dawa Samdup (Ka
dzi Zla ba bsam 'grub),
4–5, 10, 74–79, 80, 94,
99, 105–106, 116, 149–
150, 170

Koot Hoomi, 20, 74
Kübler-Ross, Elisabeth,
120, 123

Ladenla, Sardar Bahādur,
74, 78, 158
Lang, Andrew, 23
Lang Darma (Glang dar
ma), 52, 133
Leary, Timothy, 8, 158
Lebolo, Antonio, 153
Lepsius, Karl Richard,
101
Li Gotami, 90–92
Lyne, Adrian, 9

Maitreya, 115
Marpa, 53
Metzner, Ralph, 9, 158
Milarepa, 53
Moody, Raymond, 121,
123
Moroni, 14–15, 22
Morya, 20

Nāgārjuna, 136
Nāropa, 146–147
Notovitch, Nicolas, 73
Nyānaponika Mahāthera,
91
Nyānatiloka Mahāthera,
89
Nyima Drakpa. *See* Rigzin
Nyima Drakpa

Olcott, Henry Steel, 18–19, 22, 71, 150

Padmasambhava, 2, 52, 54, 56, 58–59, 66–67, 78, 96, 110, 134–135, 137–138, 150–151

Ramana Maharshi, 77
Rigzin Nyima Drakpa (Rig 'dzin nyi ma grags pa), 67–68, 124
Russell, George William, 23

Śāntarakṣita, 52
Satyananda, Swami, 71,77
Scoville, Thomas, 10
Sinnett, Alfred Percy, 19
Smith, Emma, 15, 17, 141, 143
Smith, Joseph, 14–18, 21–22, 139–144, 147–148, 150–151, 153–155, 159
Snyder, Gary, 92
Sogyal Rinpoche, 122
Songtsen Gampo (Srong btsan sgam po), 51, 54

Spiritualism, 7–8, 11, 18–19, 22, 145
Strang, James Jesse, 17, 144

Theosophical Society, 19, 21–23, 71, 76, 93
Theosophy, 19, 23–24, 27, 79, 93, 96, 101, 103, 118, 149
Thurman, Robert, 123
Tingley, Katherine, 22
Tirard, Helen Mary, 102
Tomo Geshe Rimpoche (Gro mo dge bshes rin po che), 89, 91, 94
Trisong Detsen (Khri srong sde btsan), 51, 56
Tsong kha pa, 53

Urim and Thummim, 15, 16, 149, 154

Vajrasattva, 63–65
Vedas, 129–130, 132, 133
Virūpa, 53

Woodroffe, John, 5, 96–97